W9-BSZ-702

TEST CONSTRUCTION:

A PROGRAMMED GUIDE

OBJECTIVES 15 16 17

100 A
99 B
12 13 C
D
E

LOWELL A. SCHOER

FALSE TRUE

Test Construction: A Programmed Guide

Lowell A. Schoer

THE UNIVERSITY OF IOWA

Test Construction: A Programmed Guide

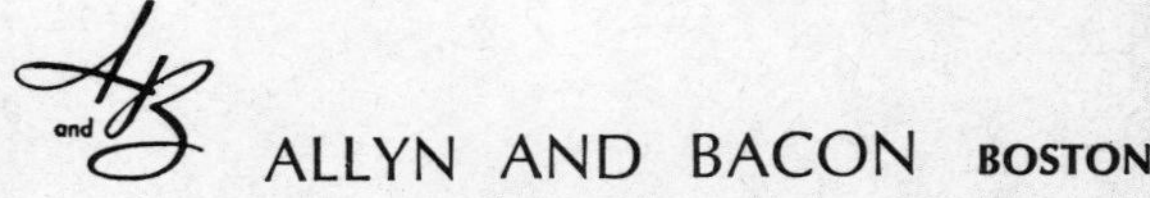

470 Atlantic Avenue, Boston, Mass.

Library of Congress Catalogue Card Number: 76-90342

Printed in the United States of America.

Table of Contents

Preface

Test construction is among the most difficult tasks teachers perform, yet many teachers have little background in the principles of item construction. There is often too little room in a training program for more than a smattering of measurement and too little time to study measurement once the teacher is on the job. This book was written to help overcome both of these problems. A programmed format was chosen so these topics could be learned quickly without benefit of a course or other outside help.

There is a section on actual item construction, but considerable emphasis is also given to the role of testing in the instructional program. Only when a teacher recognizes how testing should interact with stating objectives and teaching can he write tests which will serve the purposes for which they are intended.

To The Student

When you have finished this book you should be able to:

1. Point out the relationship among teaching, testing, and objectives.
2. Compare and contrast the roles of standardized and teacher-made tests in the measurement of classroom achievement.
3. Define the terms validity, reliability, and efficiency as they are used in testing and apply the concepts to problems in test construction.
4. Point out poorly stated objectives.
5. Write objectives in behavioral terms.
6. Define the basis for each of the major classifications in the Taxonomy of Educational Objectives.
7. Classify test items using the terminology and classification system of the Taxonomy of Educational Objectives.
8. Point out the reasons for using a table of specifications.
9. Set up a table of specifications.
10. Answer questions relative to test length and student preparation.
11. Differentiate between power and speed tests, and between supply and choice-type items.

12. Specify the advantages and disadvantages of essay, short-answer, multiple-choice, matching, and true-false items.
13. Point out errors in essay, short-answer, multiple-choice, matching, and true-false items.
14. Write essay, short-answer, multiple-choice, matching, and true-false items which are technically adequate.
15. Specify which type of item would be most useful under a given set of conditions.
16. Point out advantages and disadvantages of weighting items and correcting for guessing.
17. Set up a frequency distribution and determine percentile ranks.
18. Set up an item analysis table.
19. Compute difficulty and discrimination indices from an item analysis table.
20. Recognize factors to consider when setting up a marking system.
21. Differentiate a good marking system from a poor one.

You cannot read this book by going from page 1 to page 2 to page 3, etc., as you do with a regular text. This book is set up and must be used quite differently from most books. The first difference you will notice is that the material is divided into small units called frames and that each frame ends with a question. These questions serve two purposes. They make active participation on your part an integral part of the book, and they serve as a means of checking on whether or not you have understood what you have read. The second difference you will notice is that the page and letter you turn to after a frame depends on how you answer the question in that frame. You cannot proceed to the next major frame until you answer the question correctly. In order to derive maximum benefit from this "self correction" be sure to turn to the page indicated after the answer you have selected to the question.

You are now ready to begin. Turn to page 3, read the frame, answer the question, and turn to the page given in parentheses after your answer.

CHAPTER 1

Coordinating Teaching, Testing, and Grading with Objectives

A *I 1*

Testing serves a number of useful purposes in education: (1) It provides a basis for assigning marks which can be used to report how well the student is doing. But their educational value virtually disappears when tests are seen as necessary evils to be tacked on a course for purposes of assigning grades. In fact, they may well detract from instruction by diverting the student's attention and wasting his time. (2) Tests also exercise a strong influence on when, what, and how a student studies. When properly prepared, tests require a teacher to do some very careful thinking about his instructional objectives. In order to write tests which can serve as useful devices for motivating and directing student and teacher behavior, however, the teacher must recognize the close relationship between objectives – teaching and testing.

Which of the following statements is true?

a. Any test is better than no test at all. *(P. 4A.)*

b. The most serious outcome of a poor test is wasting the student's time. *(P. 6A.)*

c. A poor test may well have a negative effect on student learning. *(P. 8A.)*

B *I 3b*

This shows a pattern in which each of the four parts interact with the others. Should testing procedures influence teaching, or should grading practices influence objectives? They should not do either, at least to any significant degree. Return to page 7 and choose another answer.

A *I 1a*

This seems to be what is sometimes assumed when the teacher says, "Well, it's test time again. Which set of questions shall I use this year?" Unfortunately, a test put together in this way can not only waste teacher and student time, but actually misguide the student. Return to page *3* and choose another answer.

B *I 3c*

This shows only the order in which the four typically occur. There is a better answer which shows one to be the basis for each of the other three. Return to page *7* and find it.

A *I 2a*

There are some teachers who seem to take the position that testing is a game that is played between teachers and students. To them, the sign of a good test becomes "fooling the students" by giving them items very different from what they might expect. If teaching and testing are done from the same set of objectives students might not be able to anticipate specific items, but they should be able to anticipate the kinds of questions to be asked. At the very least, surprising the students is hardly a basis for calling a test a good one. Return to page *8* and choose another answer.

B *I 4b 5*

Right! Teacher-made and standardized tests serve somewhat different ends, but they do have much in common.

Two basic differences between the teacher-made test and the standardized test are the content covered and the objectives measured. Standardized tests are based on content and objectives which many school systems share in common. Teacher-made tests are generally based on more limited content and local objectives. This does not mean that teacher-made tests measure only detail and unimportant objectives. Their content and objectives may be as important as those measured by a standardized test, but they tend to be more local in orientation.

For which of the following would a teacher be most likely to have to rely on his own tests?

a. Measurement of map-reading skills. (*P. 7B.*)

b. Measurement of ability to do long division. (*P. 8B.*)

c. Measurement of knowledge about the economy of Alaska. (*P. 10B.*)

A *I 1b*

This can be a serious outcome because student and class time is valuable. It is not, however, the most serious outcome of a poor test. Return to page *3* and choose another answer.

B *I 4a*

The point was made that the study of standardized testing can make a contribution to classroom testing. It was also pointed out that standardized tests complement classroom tests. Is it likely then that they have nothing in common? Return to page *9* and choose another answer.

A *I 2b 3*

You have chosen correctly. If teaching and testing are both based on the same set of objectives, students should be able to predict the kinds of items that are likely to appear on a test on the basis of what occurs in class. Not being able to do so is certainly not an indication that a test is a good one.

Recognizing the proper relationship between teaching and testing also puts the relationship between testing and grading in the proper perspective. If the teacher sets his objectives in order, teaches to reach them, and tests to determine where students are relative to these objectives, the grade assigned on the basis of that testing should validly reflect a student's achievement. The student who gets a good grade will be the one who has achieved a high level of performance relative to the outcomes of instruction. It is only when the tests do not measure these important outcomes that getting a good grade may be unrelated to achievement.

Which of the following most accurately pictures the relationship among objectives, teaching, testing, and the assignment of grades?

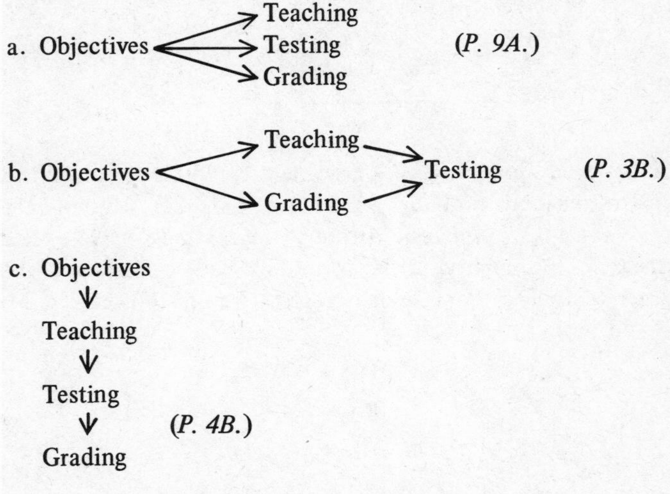

B *I 5a*

Map-reading skills are of such general use that most schools would be concerned that children acquire them. Map-reading skills then are likely to be covered in a standardized test. Although a teacher might write his own tests to measure this skill, there is another choice on page *5* for which he is more likely to have to rely on his own tests. Return to page *5* and find it.

A *I 1c 2*

You chose the correct answer: A poor test may well have a negative effect on learning.

Suppose a teacher begins a semester by saying to a class, "I am concerned that in this course you learn principles and how to apply them. Don't try to memorize a lot of facts." The students, taking him at his word, study to learn principles and applications. At the end of the third week of class, the teacher gives a test which consists of ten definitions and twenty other fact-type items. There is little question that many students will change their study habits for the next three-week period. The problem is that the teacher has one set of objectives in his teaching and uses another set when writing his tests. The proper relationship between teaching and testing requires that both be based on the same objectives.

This student reaction is an indication of a good test: "I didn't expect those kinds of items."

a. True. (*P. 5A.*)

b. False. (*P. 7A.*)

B *I 5b*

Is the ability to do long division one which would be of concern to most schools? The answer is probably affirmative. This then would likely to be covered on a standardized test. Although teachers do indeed write tests which measure this ability, there is another choice for which they are likely to rely more heavily on their own tests. Return to page *5* and find it.

A *I 3a 4*

Good! Teaching, testing, and grading all must be derived from the objectives of instruction. It is these objectives which are the heart of the instructional process, and it is only through them that teaching and testing can be properly coordinated and grading become meaningful. The importance of objectives in teaching and testing will be discussed in more detail later. For now we will leave it and take up the matter of teacher-made and standardized tests. There are two reasons for bringing standardized achievement tests into this discussion. The first is to make it very clear that these two types of tests are not competitive but complementary. The second is to show what contribution standardized testing can make to better classroom tests.

Which of the following best reflects the relationship between teacher-made and standardized tests?

a. They share almost nothing in common. (*P. 6B.*)

b. They have much in common. (*P. 5B.*)

c. They are interchangeable for most purposes. (*P. 10A.*)

B *I 6c*

There are certain characteristics of both standardized tests and the teacher-made tests which give each an advantage in certain situations. Where the comparison is from school to school as this one is, the more general content and objectives of one of these types of test makes it preferable to the other. Return to page *10* and find it.

A *I 4c*

Whoops! Although they have much in common, standardized and teacher-made tests do serve somewhat different ends. They are not interchangeable. Return to page *9* and choose another answer.

B *I 5c 6*

Right! Although the teacher might write tests covering the other two, they are sufficiently broad to be covered on standardized tests. Knowledge about the economy of Alaska is, however, too restricted an area to be covered on a standardized test. The teacher would probably have to rely on his own tests to measure it.

In addition to measuring different types of content and objectives, the results of teacher-made achievement tests and standardized achievement tests serve different purposes. Standardized achievement test scores can be used to make comparisons from class to class, building to building, or from school system to school system. They can also be used to study pupil growth or to make ability-achievement comparisons. Teacher-made achievement tests can be more validly used (1) to determine whether or not certain local objectives have been met and (2) to assign grades.

Suppose a history teacher would like to know how the achievement of his students compares with that of other students from high schools of similar size in the state. What type of test should he use?

a. A standardized test. (*P. 12A.*)

b. A teacher-made test. (*P. 14A.*)

c. One would do as well as the other. (*P. 9B.*)

A *I 7a 8*

Right! Standardized tests tend to be based on broader content and more general objectives than teacher-made tests. It is very possible that a comparison of groups using one type of test would show an advantage to one group while the results of a test of the other type would show an advantage to the other group.

We have, up to now, emphasized the differences between standardized and teacher-made tests. Except for the development of norms, however, the problems encountered in writing any achievement test are much the same, regardless of whether it is a standardized test constructed by testing specialists or a test developed by a teacher. Both begin with a careful definition of the content to be covered and the objectives to be measured. Then a decision about which type of item (essay, multiple-choice, true-false) to use must be made. This is followed by the development of a test blueprint which serves as a guide in determining how many items of which type are needed in each part of the content covered in the test. After these steps have been completed, item writing begins. Once the items have been written the test must be administered, the items analyzed, and revisions made where necessary.

Which of the following steps would be less essential in developing a teacher-made test than in developing a standardized test?

a. Careful choice of a norm group. (*P. 14B.*)

b. Careful statement of objectives. (*P. 12B.*)

c. Careful analysis and revision of items. (*P. 16A.*)

B *I 9a*

Most teachers write many tests every school year, so the problem is not that they have too little practice in test construction. There is another reason given which is more likely. Return to page *14* and find it.

A *I 6a 7*

Good! Although a teacher-made test could be used, a standardized test would be preferred.

Tests are frequently used to make comparisons between groups of students. When this is done two factors must be considered in interpreting the results. The first is differences between the groups which might give one the advantage over the other. If, for instance, the average I.Q. of one group is 90 and that for the other is 120, this difference must be considered in interpreting the scores they attain on an achievement test. This becomes particularly critical if the comparison is to be used to make judgments about teachers or methods of instruction. The second factor is the set of objectives the test was designed to measure. One group may do better than another if the test was designed to measure the recall of facts. If the test was designed to measure skill in application, the results might be very different. No test can measure everything. Performance on any test must be interpreted in terms of what that particular test measures.

Two classes each take two tests. One is a standardized test. The other is a teacher-made test. It would be very possible for one class to do better than the other on the standardized test and less well on the teacher-made test.

a. True. (*P. 11A.*)

b. False. (*P. 15A.*)

B *I 8b*

Every test should be based on a careful statement of objectives, regardless of who is writing it or for whom it is written. Return to page *11* and choose another answer.

A *I 9b 10*

Good! Teachers get plenty of practice in test construction during a school year and have ample opportunity to examine good standardized tests. The problem is knowing what a good test is and how to write one.

The first thing a good test must be is valid. It must measure what it is supposed to measure. The term "validity" has been used in an earlier frame but it is important enough to deserve specific mention once more. In achievement testing, the validity of a test is determined very largely by the degree to which the items are based on what has been taught and the degree to which they reflect the objectives of instruction. Because validity of this type depends on the content of the test, it is referred to as "content validity." Content validity is largely a matter of judgment on the part of the person making or reading the test so it can be classified as type of rational validity. Although content validity may in the final analysis be a judgment, the judgment can be made considerably more reliable if there is a very clear statement of objectives against which to judge the items.

To what does the term content validity refer?

a. Items on a test. (*P. 15B.*)

b. Content of a course. (*P. 16B.*)

B *I 11a*

Although a test like this would probably not have very high validity, there is a better answer. Return to page *15* and find it.

A *I 6b*

This is a school to school comparison. Although a teacher-made test might be used it would probably be better to use a standardized test with its emphasis on more general content and objectives. Return to page *10* and choose the correct answer.

B *I 7a 9*

Good! A statement of objectives and an item analysis are equally important in teacher-made and standardized tests. The choice of a norm group is not much of an issue with the typical teacher-made test. The students in the class in which the test is given constitute the only norm group about which the teacher is likely to be concerned.

There is little question that testing specialists have more time to prepare tests than do classroom teachers. Neither is there much question about the superiority of the facilities available to the specialist. It may also be that only people who have a special "knack" for item writing become testing specialists. There is, however, much more to writing test items than time, facilities, and a "gift." There is a body of facts and principles which, when applied, can improve the validity and reliability of any test.

Which of following is probably an important reason teachers so often write poor tests?

a. They have not had enough practice in test construction. (*P. 11B.*)

b. They do not know the basic principles of test construction. (*P. 13A.*)

c. They have never seen a really good test. (*P. 17A.*)

A *I 7b*

Standardized and teacher-made tests often are developed to measure different types of objectives. Because they measure different things two groups of students might perform very differently on them. One group might do better on one and less well on the other. Return to page *12* and choose another answer.

B *I 10a 11*

Right! As discussed, the term content validity refers to the items on a test and the degree to which they cover the content of a course and reflect the objectives of instruction.

Another important characteristic of a good test is reliability. A test must not only measure what it is supposed to measure but it must do it reliably. A test which gives widely fluctuating results from one time to another is not a good test. While content validity is determined on a rational basis, reliability is determined on a statistical basis. It generally involves some method of correlating two scores students have received on two sets of items covering the same content and based on the same objectives. Sometimes the same test is given on two different occasions. Sometimes parallel forms of a test are used. Frequently scores on two halves of the same test are used.

If a student scores near the top on a test at one time and near the middle when the test is readministered, the test would be said to lack:

a. Validity. (*P. 13B.*)

b. Reliability. (*P. 17B.*)

A

I 8c

Although this is frequently neglected in classroom tests, it should be as important a part of classroom test development as it is of standardized test development. Return to page *11* and choose another answer.

B

I 10b

Questions might be raised about the validity of the content of a course but that is not the issue of content validity as discussed on page *13*. Return to page *13* and choose another answer.

A *I 9c*

Teachers have probably taken some good tests and they have frequent opportunity to look at well-constructed standardized tests. Return to page *14* and choose another answer.

B *I 11b 12*

Good! Such a test would be said to lack reliability. This poor reliability would also, by the way, effect validity.

While validity and reliability are of primary concern, there are a number of other characteristics to be considered in classroom testing. One of these is efficiency in administering and scoring the test and in the use of student and teacher time. A test which requires long and detailed direction or one in which there is likely to be a considerable amount of confusion among the students is not a good test. Efficiency must also be considered when choosing item types. If there are few students to be tested and the test items cannot be re-used, an essay test, which can be prepared relatively quickly, might be more efficient than a multiple-choice test which takes longer to write. If, on the other hand, the class is large and the items can be re-used, a multiple-choice test which can be scored quickly might be more efficient than an essay test. Essay tests tend to use up much of the testing time in writing and since a student can think many times more quickly than he can write, essay tests are, in this way, less efficient than multiple-choice tests.

Under which of the following sets of conditions would it be most efficient to use a multiple-choice test?

a. A large class where the items will be reused. (*P. 18A.*)

b. A small class where the items will not be reused. (*P. 19A.*)

Good! Because the class is large, the scoring efficiency of the multiple-choice test is important. The fact the items can be reused reduces the seriousness of the problem presented by the time it takes to write multiple-choice items.

We have now discussed three general issues in achievement testing; the relationship of testing to teaching, the relationship between standardized and teacher-made tests, and certain characteristics of a good test.

In the pages that follow we will go through the mechanics of test construction from the specification of content and objectives to final item revision. Many of the suggestions are taken directly from the techniques and procedures used in developing standardized tests, others are simplified procedures based on those used by test specialists. A few are likely to be used only with classroom tests. Regardless of which type they are, they are all designed to help the teacher construct tests and write items which will do what the teacher wants them to do and will fit into his total pattern of teaching and testing. Turn to page *20*.

A *I 12b*

If a test does not have validity, whatever else it might have makes little difference. Although it is frequently necessary to compromise in these matters, validity must always be given primary consideration. Return to page *17* and choose another answer.

CHAPTER 2

Writing Educational Objectives

A *II 1*

When objectives are developed carefully and stated properly they provide a sound basis for choosing methods and materials for teaching, writing tests, and assigning grades. The teacher who does not spend sufficient time developing his objectives is very likely to find himself "covering material" and testing, and grading on the basis of how well students can parrot this material back to him. In such a situation methods and materials determine objectives.

If a teacher does not specify what the outcomes of instruction should be, he will not achieve any objectives.

a. True. (*P. 24A.*)

b. False. (*P. 26A.*)

B *II 2a*

Whoops! The point was made that educational objectives should not be limited to those outcomes which are easy to measure. There are, in fact, many important objectives which are extremely difficult to measure or which can be measured only indirectly. Reread the paragraph on page *26* and choose another answer.

A

II 1a

This may be somewhat of a "curve ball" question but it was written to emphasize that teaching will lead somewhere. The problem is that unless the teacher specifies his objectives and works to reach them, the objectives that will be achieved are those that occur without any special planning. Objectives that occur by chance might well be very different from those that the teacher would want. Return to page *23* and choose another answer.

B

II 2b 3

You have chosen the correct answer. Educational objectives must be stated clearly. If they are not, they can provide little guidance for teaching and testing.

Ultimately objectives should be expressed in terms of student behavior. Doing so makes objectives more useful as guides to instruction and testing. The objective, "Enhance the student's self-concept" is not expressed in behavioral terms and while it might be a valid objective, it is not a very useful one as it is expressed. The term "enhance" has many connotations and two people reading that objective might interpret it very differently. The same is true of "self-concept." What is needed is to translate this objective into behavioral terms. This requires that we define those behaviors which differentiate students with good self-concepts from students with poor ones. Although the task might be a difficult one, it must be done if the objective is to be useful. It should be emphasized that the objective should not be rejected just because it may be difficult to put in behavioral terms. It must be rejected, however, if it is impossible to put in behavioral terms.

Which of the following is the most acceptable statement of an educational objective?

a. Given pictures, the student should be able to identify the 25 most common birds found east of the Mississippi. (*P. 27A.*)

b. The student should develop an appreciation of the importance of birds in maintaining a balance of nature. (*P. 28A.*)

A *II 4a*

Do the words "write," "draw," "list," and "make speeches" specify attitudes? A certain kind of writing might reflect an attitude but the act of writing itself is another matter. Return to page *27* and choose another answer.

B *II 5b 6*

You are right! Both "compare" and "describe" refer to behaviors while "enjoy" does not. It could be made more useful by specifying what behavior defines "enjoy," but as it stands it is the least desirable of the three terms given.

Two nonbehavioral terms which have been widely used in statements of educational objectives are "know" and "understand." There are, in fact, many who would define the primary goal of education to be helping students acquire knowledge and understanding of themselves and their world. Frequently this is as far as it goes and no attempt is made to define what behaviors are associated with knowing and understanding. This very loose usage of terms has led some to insist that educational objectives must be defined only in terms of behaviors, and that terms such as "knowledge" and "understanding" serve no useful purpose.

Those who insist that the terms "knowledge" and "understanding" serve no useful purpose in a statement of educational objectives would also object to the term:

a. Explain. (*P. 29A.*)

b. Defend. (*P. 30B.*)

c. Believe. (*P. 32A.*)

A

II 1b 2

Right! Teaching will lead somewhere, i.e., it will achieve some objectives. The problem is that these objectives be those the teacher has specified and worked to achieve, not those that just happen by chance. It is not a matter of achieving or not achieving objectives, but a matter of what objectives are achieved.

If they are to serve as good bases for instruction and testing, educational objectives must show two characteristics. They must first and foremost reflect important outcomes of education. Secondly, they must be stated in unambiguous terms. The second of these is particularly critical in testing. Unless the objectives are stated very carefully, it may be extremely difficult to write a valid test from them. This does not mean that we must content ourselves only with objectives that can be measured with a minimum of effort. Despite the fact certain educational outcomes may be extremely difficult to measure we cannot, if they are important outcomes, reject them on that basis alone.

Which of the following is the more critical attribute for an educational objective?

a. It must be easily and directly measurable. (*P. 23B.*)

b. It must be stated clearly. (*P. 24B.*)

B

II 5a

Although it might be necessary to add additional qualifications to an objective which contained the word "compare," it does refer to a behavior. There is another term in the list which does not. Return to page *28* and find it.

A *II 3a 4*

Good! You recognized that this is an objective expressed in behavioral terms while the other is not. It may be important that students develop an appreciation of birds in the balance of nature but as it is stated, there are too many ill-defined words in objective *b*.

If such an appreciation is assumed to be important, the objective, as stated, might serve as a starting point. The next step would be to define the concept "balance of nature" and indicate what behaviors would be shown by a student who "appreciates" the value of birds in maintaining it. Put another way, what will a student, who appreciates the importance of birds in maintaining the balance of nature, be able or willing to do? Does it mean he can list the insects birds eat? Does it mean he can write an acceptable two-page paper on the amount of weed seeds consumed by birds? Does it mean he can draw a chart which shows animals which depend on birds for food? Does it mean he is willing to go out and make speeches in support of a local bird conservation project?

In each instance, the words which are underlined in the preceding paragraph are words which specify:

a. An attitude. (*P. 25A.*)

b. A behavior. (*P. 28B.*)

c. A value. (*P. 30A.*)

B *II 7b*

Although the word "understand" is used, it is related to behavior through specifying how he will show this understanding. Because this has been done the objective is stated in an acceptable fashion. Return to page *32* and choose another answer.

A *II 3b*

What do the words "appreciation" and "balance of nature" mean to you? Do you suppose they might mean something different to someone else? The objective might be a valid one, but the use of the words "appreciation" and "balance of nature" are open to too many different interpretations. Return to page *24* and choose another answer.

B *II 4b 5*

Right! The underlined words do specify behavior and are the type of words that must be used somewhere in the development of objectives.

Which of the following terms would be least desirable in a final statement of objectives?

a. Compare. (*P. 26B.*)

b. Enjoy. (*P. 25B.*)

c. Describe. (*P. 31A.*)

A *II 6a*

The objection to the terms "knowledge" and "understanding" is that they are nonbehavioral. "Explain" describes a behavior so it would not be objectionable. One of the words on page *25* is nonbehavioral. Return and find it.

B *II 7a 8*

Good! You recognized that specifying the behaviors to be used as evidence of understanding makes expression of the objective acceptable.

Bloom et al. have prepared a Taxonomy of Educational Objectives in the cognitive domain (that of knowing and understanding) which is extremely useful in helping teachers think more precisely in this area. Although it is process-oriented, care is taken to specify what kinds of behaviors might be used to measure certain processes. Because of the way it was prepared the Taxonomy can be a valuable aid to the teacher in helping him clarify his thinking about objectives and in writing test items.

Which of the following best describes the Taxonomy of Educational Objectives?

a. It is a listing of methods and techniques useful in teaching knowledge and understanding. (*P. 32B.*)

b. It is a classification of processes and behaviors which reflect knowledge and understanding. (*P. 31B.*)

A *II 4c*

Do the words, "list," "write," "draw," and "make speeches" specify values? What kinds of speeches a person makes might be used to infer his values but making speeches as such falls under one of the other answers. Return to page *27* and find it.

B *II 6b*

"Defend" refers to a behavior so it would not be objectionable to those who reject "knowledge" and "understanding" because they are nonbehavioral. Return to page *25* and choose another answer.

A *II 5c*

Does "describe" refer to a behavior? Is there another term in the list which does not? The answer to both questions is "yes." Return to page *28* and find the term which does not refer to a behavior.

B *II 8b 9*

Good! The Taxonomy of Educational Objectives is a classification of processes and behaviors which reflect them.

The Taxonomy sets up six major classifications in the cognitive domain. They are knowledge, comprehension, application, analysis, synthesis, and evaluation. In the knowledge classification the student must recognize or recall what he has learned. The response the student makes in the test situation is the same one he made or heard while learning. This means, of course, that whether a given question is a knowledge-type question or not depends not only on the nature of the question but also on what has occurred in the classroom. A given question may be knowledge-type question for one group of students but not for another.

Suppose a teacher puts the following question on a test: "How is Thomas Jefferson's political philosophy reflected in the American Constitution?" Is this a knowledge-type question?

a. Yes. (*P. 33A.*)

b. No. (*P. 34A.*)

c. No way to tell from what is given. (*P. 36A.*)

A *II 6c 7*

Good! Those who object to "knowledge" and "understanding" do so because the terms are nonbehavioral. They would object to "believe" for the same reason.

While the view that all educational objectives must be expressed in behavioral terms has a good deal of merit there is a danger with it. The danger is that too much emphasis can be put on product and conditioning and not enough on process and thinking. The difficulty with the terms "knowledge" and "understanding" is that they are so ambiguous. It is possible to reduce this ambiguity without having to do away with the concepts completely. What is required is that we specify the types of behaviors that are related to knowledge and understanding. Ultimately, objectives must be related to behaviors and these behaviors must be specified, but that does not necessarily mean that concepts such as knowledge, understanding, and appreciation have no place anywhere in the development of a list of educational objectives.

A teacher writes the following as an objective: "The student should understand the causes of the War of 1812 and show this understanding by being able to write about them in his own words, discuss them in class, and relate them to the causes of other wars in American history."

Is this objective stated in an acceptable fashion?

a. Yes. (*P. 29B.*)

b. No. (*P. 27B.*)

B *II 8a*

You have missed the point of the material presented on page *29*. Return to page *29* reread the material and choose another answer.

A *II 9a*

It would be a knowledge-type question if the relationship asked for had been discussed in class, and the student was expected to remember and put down what had been said. From what is given on page *31* do you know whether or not this was the case? Return to page *31* and choose another answer.

B *II 10a*

This question does not require the student to translate something from one form into another. He is not asked to paraphrase or summarize but to predict direction. Return to page *36* and choose another answer.

A *II 9b*

Do you have any way of knowing whether or not the relationship between Jefferson's political philosophy and the American Constitution had been discussed in class? If it had not been, your answer is the correct one. If it had been, however, and the student was expected to write down what he remembered of the discussion, this would be a knowledge-type question. Return to page *31* and choose another answer.

B *II 11a*

The point was made on page *38* that "knowing" and "understanding" do not assure "applying." There are many instances where students may know and understand a principle but yet not be able to apply it in a concrete situation. Return to page *38* and choose another answer.

A *II 10b*

The student is not asked to explain or summarize certain events in the history of music in America; he is asked to predict from them. Return to page *36* and choose another answer.

B *II 12a 13*

Good! Synthesis requires the student to combine many elements into a whole. Although the value placed on the uniqueness of this whole may be greater in a unit on "Creative Writing" than in one on "Science in American Life," synthesis is in either case more closely related to creativity than is analysis.

Evaluation is the last of the processes discussed in the Taxonomy of Educational Objectives. It refers to making judgments about worth. Such judgments may be made on the basis of internal evidence such as how logically a selection is organized or how carefully the facts seem to be reported. It may also be made on the basis of external evidence such as how consistent it is with other things the student has heard or read.

Analyzing a selection to determine whether or not the conclusions follow from the evidence cited is an example of using an:

a. Internal criterion. *(P 37A.)*

b. External criterion. *(P. 39A.)*

You are right! The only way to tell if it is a knowledge-type item would be to know whether or not the relationship between Jefferson's political philosophy and the American Constitution had been discussed in class. If it had been and the student had only to remember what had been said to answer the question, it is a knowledge-type item. If it had not been discussed, however, and the answer required more than memory, it would not be a knowledge-type question.

Comprehension, while it involves knowledge, goes beyond remembering to being able to perform certain operations with a communication beyond recalling or reproducing it. The Taxonomy lists three types of behaviors which reflect comprehension. They are translation, interpretation, and extrapolation. Asking a student to take an abstract idea and express it in his own words or asking him to transform a verbal statement into an algebraic equation are examples of translation. In interpretation the student is required not only to rephrase, but to explain or give the meaning of the communication. Extrapolation requires him to make certain predictions or draw certain implications that go beyond the present communication.

A teacher put the following question on a test: "On the basis of what we have studied about the history of music in America, what direction do you think it will take in the future?" What type of behavior does this question require of the students?

a. Translation. (*P. 33B.*)

b. Interpretation. (*P. 35A.*)

c. Extrapolation. (*P. 38A.*)

A *II 13a*

Right! The logic of the presentation is an internal criterion. It relates to internal structure rather than to the degree to which the selection conforms to external criteria, such as style and technique.

The Taxonomy of Educational Objectives is not the final answer to problems of developing useful objectives of instruction. It was used in this section as an example of how objectives can be classified and test items developed from them. It was not presented as a prescription to be followed by all teachers at all times. Each teacher must use his own judgment and adjust the Taxonomy to meet his particular needs.

A considerable amount of time has been spent in this chapter on objectives, but unless the teacher recognizes the importance of carefully thought out and precisely stated objectives, he cannot write a good test no matter how technically well done it might be. Turn to page *43*.

B *II 11b 12*

Correct! Students can know and understand a principle, yet not be able to apply it in concrete situations. Because this is true, the teacher must show students how principles can be applied to concrete situations while he is teaching and test for the student's ability to apply what he knows when he is testing.

Analysis involves taking a whole and breaking it down into its parts. Synthesis involves taking parts and combining them into a whole. In analysis the object is to determine the relationship of the parts to each other and see how they form the whole. In synthesis the object is to create a new whole out of the parts that are available. Giving students a short essay and asking them to pick out the important thought, relationships, and organizational principles would be an example of synthesis.

"Creativity" is most closely related to:

a. Synthesis. (*P. 35B.*)

b. Analysis. (*P. 38B.*)

A *II 10c 11*

Good! The student is asked to predict what he thinks will occur on the basis of what he knows about the history of music in America. This is extrapolation.

Application-type items are exactly what their name implies. They are items which require the student to apply what he knows. We must be concerned about application because so much of what is learned in school has little significance unless the student can use it in concrete situations. There is ample evidence that knowing and understanding do not assure application outside the confines of the classroom.

If a student knows and understands a principle he can probably apply it.

a. True. (*P. 34B.*)

b. False. (*P. 37B.*)

B *II 12b*

In analysis the student starts with a whole, such as an essay, a play, or a formula and breaks it down into parts. In synthesis the student is required to make the whole from the parts he has available. Which involves creating something? Return to page *37*, reread the paragraph, and choose another answer.

Although the fact that conclusions should be based directly on evidence cited may be something a student has learned previously and in that sense be external, the internal structure is what is being analyzed. Return to page *35* and choose another answer.

CHAPTER *3*

Developing a Table of Specifications

A *III 1*

A test, if it is to be valid, must be based on the objectives of instruction and the content covered in the course. We have spent considerable time discussing objectives but we should not forget the content outline as a part of test planning. The outlining should be done in enough detail so that no major points are omitted, but need not include every point that has been covered in class. The purpose of the outline is to be sure that the test is comprehensive and does not weight certain areas too heavily at the expense of other equally important ones. There are certain types of content on which it is much easier to write items than others. If the teacher does not have an outline to guide him, the test may well cover only these areas.

Which of the following is most likely to result from not preparing a content outline prior to writing a test?

a. Too many items on a relatively minor point. (*P. 44A.*)

b. Items which measure relatively unimportant outcomes. (*P. 46A.*)

c. Use of the wrong types of items. (*P. 48A.*)

B *III 2a*

Forty percent of the items are to come from unit III. Does 40 percent of 80 equal 8? Multiply .4 X 80 and return to page *44* and choose the correct answer.

A *III 1a 2*

Right! Failure to prepare a careful outline of the content to be covered on the test may well result in writing a number of items on a relatively minor point because it is easy to write items on that point.

The blueprint for a test is called a table of specifications. One of the easiest ways to set up a table of specifications is to make a two-way table with the general content areas across the top and the general objectives down the side. An example of what the top of such a table might look like is shown below.

CONTENT			
I	II	III	IV
(20%)	(30%)	(40%)	(10%)

The material to be covered in the test for which this table is to be used is divided into four major units. The values under the I, II, III, and IV assign the weights to each. The basis for this assignment of weight is the teacher's judgment about the importance of each unit. Although the number of pages read or the class hours spent would presumably be related to the weight assigned, these need not be the only criteria used. Using these weights, a 50-item test would have 10 items from unit I (20 percent of 50 is 10), 15 from unit II, 20 from unit III, and 5 from unit IV.

How many items would come from unit III if the test contained 80 items?

a. 8. (*P. 43B.*)

b. 32. (*P. 46B.*)

c. 40. (*P. 49A.*)

B *III 6a*

This objective, as it is stated, represents the general objective, "can define and use terminology correctly" as it might be applied to two specific terms from one of the units of content covered on a test. The objectives to be placed down the side of a table of specifications should be in general form rather than making a specific reference to material from a given unit of content. Return to page *47* and choose another answer.

A *III 3a*

Objective *D* is weighted 20 percent. Does 20 percent of 60 equal 6? Return to page *46* and choose another response.

B *III 4a 5*

Good! 30 percent of the 60 items should come from unit II and 20 percent of these 18 should be based on objective *D*. That makes 3.6 (.20 X 18 = 3.6) which means that 3 or 4 of the items which come from unit II should be based on objective *D*.

Once the table has been set up, this same procedure can be used to determine the number of items based on each objective which are required for every unit covered. The same table can be used for any length of test. It is not restricted to 1 of 60 items. Just to give you a little more practice in using it, suppose you were writing a 100-item test. How many items based on objective *B* should come from unit IV? (The table is on page *48*.)

a. 3. (*P. 47B.*)

b. 10. (*P. 49B.*)

c. 30. (*P. 50B.*)

A *III 1b*

This is more likely to be the result of not having a carefully stated set of objectives. Return to page *43* and choose another answer.

B *III 2b 3*

You are right! Forty percent of the items are to come from unit III and 40 percent of 80 is 32 (.40 X 80 = 32).

A table of specifications also includes the objectives of instruction. These can be placed down the side. This is illustrated below using the letters *A, B, C, D,* and *E* to stand for objectives.

Objectives	A	(10%)
	B	(30%)
	C	(30%)
	D	(20%)
	E	(10%)

The values in the parentheses mean the same thing here they did for content. They indicate the weight assigned each type of objective. If *A* stands for "can define and use terminology" then 10 percent of the items should require the student to define and use terminology. Similarly, 30 percent of the items should measure objective *B*, 30 percent objective *C*, 20 percent objective *D*, and 10 percent objective *E*.

If the test is to have 60 items, how many should be based on objective *D*?

a. 6. (*P. 45A.*)

b. 12. (*P. 48B.*)

c. 20. (*P. 50A.*)

A *III 4b*

There are 60 items in the test. While it is true that 12 of these should be based on objective *D* (.20 X 60 = 12), these 12 are not all from unit II. It is easier to start with the weight assigned the content unit and determine how many items should come from that unit and then find out how many of these should be based on a particular objective. In this case 18 items should come from unit II (.30 X 60 = 18) and 20 percent of these 18 should be based on objective *D*. Do it in this way, return to page *48* and choose the correct answer.

B *III 5a 6*

You have answered correctly! Ten items would come from unit IV (.10 X 100 = 10) and 30 percent or 3 of these would be based on objective *B*.

Before leaving this topic we should, perhaps, be somewhat more specific. The meaning of <u>units of instruction</u> is not likely to cause any problem. They are the major headings that would appear in a course outline. The objectives must, in order to fit across all units of instruction, be general objectives. This does not mean vague. An objective such as, "The student should understand physics," is as useless here as it would be anywhere. What is needed are objectives stated in concrete and usable form such as, "can <u>define</u> and <u>use</u> terminology correctly," or "can <u>apply</u> principles in concrete situations." What the specific term or principle is will vary from one unit to the next but the general objective remains the same across all units. The objectives can be expressed in terms of "knowing" and "understanding" but as has been indicated earlier, these terms must be defined by certain types of behavior which differentiate those who know and understand from those who do not. It is here that terms such as "define," "use," and "apply" become necessary.

Would an objective such as, "Can define and use the terms 'acid' and 'base' correctly" be in the proper form to appear as one of those listed down the side of a table of specifications?

a. Yes. (*P. 44B.*)

b. No. (*P. 51A.*)

A *III 1c*

This is more likely to be associated with poor statement of objectives. Return to page *43* and choose another answer.

B *III 3b 4*

Fine! Objective *D* is weighted 20 percent, which means on a 60-item test, 12 items should be based on this objective (.20 X 60 = 12).

Now that we have considered content and objectives separately, let us put them together in a single table. We have used Roman numerals to indicate units of content and capital letters to indicate objectives so as to keep the discussion as general as possible.

CONTENT

	I (20%)	II (30%)	III (40%)	IV (10%)
A (10%)				
B (30%)				
C (30%)				
D (20%)				
E (10%)				

To show how this table is used we will assume that we are writing a 60-item test. What has been said before means that 12 items will come from unit I (.20 X 60 = 12), 18 will come from unit 2 (.30 X 60 = 18), 24 will come from unit III (.40 X 60 = 24) and 6 will come from unit IV (.10 X 60 = 6). Now the question is, what should those 12 items from unit I be like? This is answered by looking down the row of objectives. Ten percent of them should be based on objective *A*, 30 percent on *B*, 30 percent on *C*, 20 percent on *D*, and 10 percent on *E*. 10 percent of 12 is 1.2. You cannot write .2 of an item, so let us say that 1 or 2 of the items from unit I should be based on objective *A*. Using this same method we can see that 3 or 4 should be based on objective *B* (.30 X 12 = 3.6), 3 or 4 on objective *C*, 2 or 3 on objective *D*, and 1 or 2 on objective *E*.

If this same process were followed with unit II, how many items from unit II should be based on objective *D* in a 60-item test?

a. 3 or 4. *(P. 45B.)*

b. 12 or 13. *(P. 47A.)*

c. 17 or 18. *(P. 52A.)*

A *III 2c*

The 40 under III is 40 percent. Does 40 percent of 80 equal 40? Return to page *44* and choose another answer.

B *III 5b*

Whoops! The answer you have given is the number of items that should come from unit IV (.10 X 100 = 10), but not all these should be based on objective *B*. Take another look at the table on page *48*, then return to page *45*, and choose another answer.

A *III 3c*

According to the values given, 20 percent of the items should measure objective *D*. Does 20 percent of 60 equal 20? Return to page *46* and choose another answer.

B *III 5c*

What you have done is determine the number of items that should be based on objective *B* (.30 X 100 = 30). You can get the right answer to the question this way but not all the questions based on objective *B* come from unit IV. It is easier to start from the number of items from a unit and then determine what percent of this number should be based on a certain objective. Return to page *45* and determine your answer this way.

A *III 6b 7*

You are right! The reason is that the objective, as stated, is not a general objective that could provide a basis for testing across a number of units of content. It relates to terms from one unit of content. For test purposes, these would be instances of a more general objective such as, "can define and use terms correctly." The objectives placed down the side of a table of specifications should be in this general form.

A list of objectives that might be put down the side of a table of specifications is given below. Read through the list and pick out the one you think is stated improperly.

A. Can define terms.
B. Can identify men and places.
C. Can use concepts.
D. Can apply principles.
E. Can appreciate democratic process.
F. Can state generalizations.

Turn to page *52B.*

B *III 8a*

Right! Forty percent of the items would be application-type items and 15 percent of this 40 percent would come from Chapter 2. Forty percent of 100 is 40 and 15 percent of 40 is 6. Go on to page *57*.

A *III 4c*

You are right as far as you went, but you forgot one step. While it is true that 18 items should come from unit II (.30 X 60 = 18) all should not be based on objective *D*. Only 20 percent of the 18 should be. Take this next step, return to page *48*, and choose the correct answer.

B *III 8*

Objective *E* is the one which is stated improperly. The term "appreciate" is too vague and ambiguous to be useful in this context.

An abbreviated table of specifications for a test on this book is given below.

CONTENT (by chapter)

	1 (10%)	2 (15%)	3 (10%)	4 (10%)	5 (30%)	6 (10%)	7 (15%)
A Can define terms. (10%)							
B Can recall principles. (20%)							
C Can point out similarities and differences. (10%)							
D Can apply concepts and generalizations. (40%)							
E Can analyze material. (10%)							
F Can defend certain testing procedures. (10%)							

If a test is to have 100 items, how many of them should require the student to apply concepts and generalizations presented in Chapter 2?

a. 6. (*P. 51B.*)

b. 15. (*P. 53A.*)

Fifteen would come from Chapter 2 but not all these would be application-type items. Return to page *52* and check what percentage of these 15 would be of this type. Then choose another answer.

CHAPTER 4

Making Some Preliminary Decisions

A *IV 1*

Before beginning the discussion of item construction as such we will spend time discussing some general issues that influence item writing regardless of what type of item is used.

One of these is mastery versus discriminatory testing. A mastery test is one which is written to determine whether or not a student has reached a certain level of achievement. Because of the nature of educational objectives and academic achievement, it is difficult to justify the use of mastery tests in very many classroom testing situations. Educational objectives are not typically stated in such a fashion that it is possible to specify exactly how many correct answers reflect satisfactory performance. Academic achievement tends to be more a matter of degree than of achieving or not achieving, mastery or ignorance.

The primary consideration in writing mastery tests is to

a. Spread students out as much as possible along some scale of achievement. (*P. 58A.*)

b. Differentiate those students who have reached a certain achievement level from those who have not. (*P. 60A.*)

B *IV 2a*

A mastery test typically is an either-or type test. The teacher here is using six categories which go beyond just indicating pass or fail. Return to page *60* and choose another answer.

A *IV 1a*

The primary concern in a mastery test is to classify students on the basis of whether or not they score above or below a cut-off point. The primary consideration is this cut-off point not the range of scores. Return to page *57* and choose another answer.

B *IV 2b 3*

Good! Because the test is used to assign many different grades it does not fit the description of the mastery test as we have discussed it.

In the mastery test the concern is that the items reliably discriminate between those who have reached a certain minimum level and those who have not. In a discriminatory test, there is concern with the degree to which the items rank order the students reliably at all levels. The items must be such that we can have confidence in the rank order which occurs. If the same test or a parallel form of the same test were administered later, the rank ordering should be approximately the same.

How does the problem of discrimination vary from the mastery test to the discriminatory test?

a. It is no problem with the mastery test. (*P. 61A.*)

b. It occurs at more points on the discriminatory test. (*P. 62A.*)

c. It is no problem with the discriminatory test. (*P. 64A.*)

A *IV 4a 5*

You are right! Maximum discrimination would occur on an item if 100 percent of the high achievers and 0 percent of the low achievers answered it correctly. It is not very often an item will do this, but it does, from a discrimination point of view, represent an ideal.

Another issue that must be considered in item writing is speed versus power. In a power test the primary concern is with how many items a student can answer correctly. In a speed test the primary concern is how quickly he can answer. In general, educational objectives place much more emphasis on power than on speed. This means that most classroom tests should not place too high a premium on speed, but be of such a length that most students will be able to finish all the items in the test. It is not necessary to allow time for everyone to finish, but if more than 10 percent of the students are not finished at the end of the test period, speed may be playing a more important role in determining test scores than is desirable.

Teachers should write tests so that no more than 50 percent of the students can finish all the items.

a. True. (*P. 61B.*)

b. False. (*P. 63A.*)

B *IV 7a*

The point was made that no item type is intrinsically better and therefore to be preferred above all others. This includes the essay item. Return to page *64* and choose another answer.

A *IV 1b 2*

Right! The primary consideration in a mastery test is the cut-off point not the overall spread of scores.

The cut-off point in a mastery test is often arbitrarily set by the test constructor. In a second type of test the student is categorized not on the basis of scoring above or below a certain score, but in terms of where his score lies relative to those of others like him. Such a test results in more than two (pass and fail) categories. It may, if rank in class is used, yield as many categories as there are students. Often, however, the scores are grouped into categories such as *A, B, C, D,* and *F* for excellent, good, fair, poor, and failing.

A teacher uses a test to assign grades of 95, 90, 85, 80, 75, and 70. Does this suggest he is using mastery as a basis for assigning grades?

a. Yes. (*P. 57B.*)

b. No. (*P. 58B.*)

B *IV 4b*

Discrimination refers to the degree to which the performance of high achievers exceeds that of low achievers on an item. If we had 50 high achievers and 50 low achievers when would the maximum difference in performance between these two groups occur? Would it be when 50 percent of the high achievers and 0 percent of the low achievers answered the item correctly? Return to page *62* and choose another answer.

A *IV 3a*

The mastery test must discriminate between those who have reached a certain level of achievement and those who have not. Return to page *58* and choose another answer.

B *IV 5a*

If only 50 percent of the students finish the test, the test places too much emphasis on speed for most classroom testing purposes. Return to page *59* and choose another answer.

Fine! Discrimination is a concern in both types of tests, but because of the greater number of categories involved it is a problem at more points in the discriminatory-type test than in the mastery-type test.

Technically, the term discrimination is used in measurement to refer to the degree to which high achievers answer an item correctly and low achievers do not. If a discriminatory-type test is to rank order students reliably, the individual items on that test must show this type of discrimination regardless of what type of item is used. It is as important with essay or completion items as it is with multiple-choice or true-false items.

From a discrimination point of view, an ideal item would be one which:

a. 100 percent of the high achievers and 0 percent of the low achievers answered correctly. (*P. 59A.*)

b. 50 percent of the high achievers and 0 percent of the low achievers answered correctly. (*P. 60B.*)

c. 50 percent of the high achievers and 50 percent of the low achievers answered correctly. (*P. 65A.*)

A *IV 5b 6*

Good! A test which only 50 percent of the students finish places more emphasis on speed than is desirable for most classroom testing.

One of the most important decisions to be made when writing a test is what type of item to use. Should a teacher use essay, multiple-choice, completion, matching, or true-false? Should he use only one type or a number of different types? If more than one, how many more? There is little advantage to using four or five different types of items in a test. Each time a new item type appears the student must read directions and shift his answering set. This is likely to take more time and require more adjustment on the part of the student than is desirable. If a teacher gives the matter careful thought and is willing to spend some time in item preparation, there is rarely any reason to use more than one or two types of items on a given test. While it is true that certain types of items might be particularly useful for measuring certain types of objectives, item types such as the essay and the multiple-choice can be used to measure a wide range of objectives.

If a teacher has a table of specifications which contains six major objectives how many different types of items is he likely to need on his test?

a. He will probably need no more than one or two types. (*P. 64 B.*)

b. He will probably need at least four or five types. (*P. 66A.*)

B *IV 7b*

No item type, including the multiple-choice, is intrinsically better and therefore preferable to all others. Return to page *64* and choose another answer.

A *IV 3c*

You are not reading very carefully. Return to page *58*, reread the material, and choose another answer.

B *IV 6a 7*

Good! It is very likely, one or two types of items can serve to cover these six objectives.

Which one or two the teacher will use depends on the nature of his objectives, with consideration also given to problems of reliability and economy. There is no one type of item which is intrinsically better than all others. Each has certain advantages and disadvantages. It is only when the teacher knows what these are that he can make the proper decision about what type of item to use for a given purpose.

Which of the following statements is most accurate?

a. A teacher should use essay items whenever possible and use other types only when absolutely necessary. (*P. 59B.*)

b. A teacher should use multiple-choice items whenever possible and use other types only when absolutely necessary. (*P. 63B.*)

c. It is not possible to justify the position that any type of item is so superior it should always be given preference over all others. (*P. 66B.*)

A *IV 4c*

If we had 50 high and 50 low achievers and 50 percent of each group answered an item correctly does that item discriminate between the two groups? Return to page *62* and choose another answer.

A *IV 6b*

He may, under very unusual circumstances, need as many as four but this is not likely. Chances are very good that one type of item might be used to measure many if not all six of the major objectives. Return to page *63* and choose another answer.

B *IV 7b 8*

Right! It is not possible to say one type of item is so superior to all others that it should be used whenever possible. Certain item types are more versatile than others but not to the degree that they should always be given first consideration.

A number of item types will be discussed in some detail in the next chapter. These types might be classified as belonging to one of two general types. Supply-type items are those in which the student must provide the response himself. Choice-type items are those in which the student chooses a response from a list of alternatives. Supply-type items have the advantage of being a very direct way to measure certain types of objectives. They also reduce the guessing factor and are relatively easy to write. A major disadvantage with supply-type items is relatively low reliability in scoring and poor economy in the use of student and teacher time. Choice-type items reduce the possibility of a student "answering around" a question and eliminate the effect of handwriting and skill in expression on his score. They also provide a wide sampling of behavior (many items) and can be scored quickly and reliably.

With this as background you are ready to begin Chapter 5. Turn to page *69.*

CHAPTER 5

Writing the Items

The first group of items we will consider are the supply-type. These, as you will remember, are items where the student must provide his own answer. Among the most widely used of the supply-type items is the essay question. Although it meets our definition of supply-type item, the essay question is a very special supply-type item. It is special first of all in the length of the response it requires. It is also special in the objectives which it can measure. It is not just a long fill-in-the-blank but can be used to measure objectives which cannot be measured by other supply-type items. The essay item is, in fact, often put in a category all by itself but for purpose of convenience we will include it as a supply-type item. Essay items can be used to measure almost any objective but are uniquely valuable in measuring a student's ability to write. Essay items are relatively easy to construct and allow the student considerable freedom in writing his answers. Among the major disadvantages of the essay item are the limited number of questions which can be asked during a test period, the amount of student time required to write out the answer and scoring reliability.

Which of the following most accurately describes the essay item?

a. It makes efficient use of student time. (*P. 70A.*)

b. It is uniquely useful for some purposes. (*P. 72A.*)

c. It is easy to score reliably. (*P. 74A.*)

A *V 1a*

A student can think much faster than he can write, so the essay item does not make very efficient use of student time. It may be relatively easy to write, but scoring is very time-consuming, so it does not, except when class enrollment is very small, make very efficient use of teacher time. Return to page *69* and choose another answer.

B *V 3b*

Students should be told how the items are to be weighted in the scoring and there is no reason why this cannot be put directly on the test paper. Return to page *76* and choose another answer.

A *V 2a*

An 85-point range in an essay test may be due simply to the choice of weights a teacher has used in scoring items. It says very little about how stable the scores might be. Return to page *72* and choose another answer.

B *V 4a*

It is unlikely that the mechanics of writing are emphasized this much in instruction in most courses. If they are not, there is little justification for weighting them this heavily on a test. Return to page *74* and choose another answer.

A *V 1b 2*

Right! The essay test is uniquely useful for measuring a student's ability to write.

Like any test item, essay items must measure important objectives, and they must discriminate among students. Because of the degree of freedom allowed the student in responding to an essay item, the teacher must be very careful to state the question very clearly. If the question is not stated clearly, students may interpret it differently. When this occurs it becomes difficult to know just what the question is measuring. Lack of discrimination is sometimes hidden by the way scores are assigned on essay tests. Because of the relatively arbitrary way values can be assigned essay answers, a teacher may have a range from 10 to 100 on a test and still have little real difference between the quality of the answers at these two score values. If the paper assigned the 100 is not really much different from the one assigned the 10, the items are not very discriminating no matter what values the answers are assigned.

What does a range of scores from 40-125 suggest about an essay test?

a. The test has high reliability. (*P. 71A.*)

b. The test measures important objectives. (*P. 75A.*)

c. Such a range does not necessarily suggest either of the above. (*P. 76A.*)

B *V 6a*

He can get an overview, but there is a real question of how good it is because of the possibility of one very good or one very poor answer coloring his evaluation of the others. Return to page 77 and choose another answer.

A *V 3a*

If the questions are sufficiently specific there is no reason why 3 questions are too many for a single test period. Return to page *76* and choose another answer.

B *V 4b 5*

Right! The mechanics of writing should be weighted this heavily only if they have received considerable emphasis in instruction. This is likely to occur in only a few courses.

It is very difficult to score essay items with any high degree of reliability. One important procedure in reducing unreliability of scoring is writing out a model answer. This model answer should indicate very clearly what differentiates a good answer from a poor one. Another way to reduce unreliability is to break the scoring down into a number of categories and assign scores for each category rather than use a single global score. The problem with this is that if the categories become very clear-cut and specific the scores assigned may not reflect the more general ability which was the basis for the decision to use essay items in the first place.

What is a major problem to be faced when deciding whether to assign a single global score or a large number of specific scores on an essay item?

a. Specific scores are likely to increase validity but may decrease reliability. (*P. 75B.*)

b. Specific scores are likely to increase reliability but may decrease validity. (*P. 77A.*)

A *V 1c*

Essay tests are very difficult to score reliably. Performance on essay tests, because of the requirements it puts on the student, may also be unreliable. Return to page *69* and choose another answer.

B *V 3c 4*

Correct! In general, it is better testing procedure to have all the students answer all the questions.

It is also useful to give students some direct advice on taking essay tests. This advice should include general tips as well as suggestions based directly on a particular test. They should be reminded to read each question carefully and be sure they know what it is before they start preparing an answer. They should also be told to write as legibly as possible and should be informed about the weighting to be given spelling, punctuation, and other mechanics of written expression. Some weighting may be given such mechanics, but there is a question of the validity of weighting them very heavily unless a conscious effort has been made to teach them in class.

The mechanics of writing should account for at least 25 percent of a student's score on most essay tests.

a. True. (*P. 71B.*)

b. False. (*P. 73B.*)

A *V 2b*

Is there any way to tell from the range of scores whether or not the test measures important objectives? To do this you would have to see the items. Return to page *72* and choose another answer.

B *V 5a*

The point was made that breaking scoring down into many specific categories may result in a scoring procedure which does not "get at" the general ability the test was designed to measure. This is a problem of decreased validity. Return to page *73* and choose another answer.

A *V 2c 3*

Good! The range of scores suggests very little about either the reliability or the validity of an essay test.

Although the teacher may, on occasion, wish to give a one-item essay test it is preferable to use a number of short questions rather than a single long one. Using a number of short questions has two advantages. It enables the teacher to cover a number of areas, and it makes scoring considerably easier. When a number of questions are used, the student should be told how they are to be weighted and all students should be required to answer all questions. It is difficult enough to score essay items when the students have all taken the same test (answered the same questions). It becomes even more difficult if they have taken different tests (answered different questions).

A teacher prepared a four-item essay test. The weights to be assigned each item were indicated by the question and the students were told to answer 3 of the 4. What about this test is the least defensible from a measurement point of view?

a. Having to answer 3 essay items in a test period. (*P. 73A.*)

b. Having the weights on the test paper. (*P. 70B.*)

c. Having students answer 3 of 4 questions. (*P. 74B.*)

B *V 7b*

The first question is too broad and general. The second limits the answer to the tactics of Lee and Grant and provides the student with a much better idea of what the teacher wants. Scoring is also likely to be much easier with the second than with the first question. Return to page *78* and do *c*.

A *V 5b 6*

Right! Breaking the scoring of an essay item down into categories may well increase reliability, but may also decrease validity.

Once the decision is made about what constitutes a good answer to the question and a model answer has been written, the teacher is ready to begin scoring. One big problem here is the effect which can carry over from other work the student has done in class or the way he answers the first question on the test. This can be reduced by scoring the answers as anonymously as possible and by scoring item by item instead of student by student. Although anonymity cannot be assured it can be increased by numbering tests and having students put their names and numbers on a sheet of paper. All the teacher has on the test when he scores it is a number. The name is added after the scoring is completed. Scoring item by item means scoring all the answers to question 1 at one time, then scoring all the answers to 2, etc. The advantage is that how a student answers question 1 is less likely to influence the score he gets on 2 if this procedure is followed than if his answers on 1 and 2 are scored one after the other.

Three teacher comments are given below. Which of them is most consistent with the suggestions above?

a. "I like to read all the student's answers at one time so I can get a good overview of what he knows." (*P. 72B.*)

b. "I can do a better job of scoring a test if I don't know whose paper I am reading." (*P. 78A.*)

c. "I find that the time it takes to separate the test papers, item by item, is time I could use more profitably in scoring." (*P. 80A.*)

B *V 8a*

This question is so broad as to be almost meaningless. The range of answers which could be given is so wide as to provide little or no common ground to be used as a basis for scoring. Return to page *82* and do *b*.

A *V 6b 7*

Right! The test should be scored on its own merits, not on the basis of how it fits with other impressions we might have of the student involved.

Pairs of essay items are given below. Choose the one in each pair you think is the better question. Then turn to the page given in parenthesis following that pair.

a. 1. Should we go to the metric system in the United States?
   2. What are the advantages of the metric system? (*P. 88A.*)

b. 1. Describe the Battle of Gettysburg.
   2. Compare and contrast the tactics of Lee and Grant at the Battle of Gettysburg. (*P. 76B.*)

c. 1. How are Swift's political views reflected in Gulliver's Travels?
   2. How may an author's political views be reflected in his writing? (*P. 81A.*)

d. 1. What are the essential differences between an insect and an arachnid?
   2. Name 5 insects. (*P. 84A.*)

e. 1. List the 3 rules the author of your text gives for scoring essay items.
   2. How are the scoring problems on the essay item similar to those on the completion item? (*P. 86A.*)

f. 1. What steps must be followed to amend the Constitution of the United States?
   2. Give the dates and a general description of the last 4 amendments to our Constitution. (*P. 82A.*)

B *V 8b*

There is little need to use an essay item to ask this kind of question. In fact, since the specific rules would be likely to vary from one text to another, there is little validity to such a question no matter in what form it is asked. Return to page *82* and do *c*.

A *V 9a*

A high school student can answer 4 or 5 relatively specific essay items in an hour. He can answer 60 or 70 short-answer items in the same period of time. In addition, much of the test period on an essay test is spent writing. Little time is spent writing out the answer on a short-answer test. Return to page *80* and choose another answer.

B *V 10a*

The essay item often requires the student to organize and write out relatively lengthy answers to general questions. The short-answer item typically requires him to fill in a single word or phrase to a very specific question. Does it seem to you that these different requirements would measure the same types of objectives? Return to page *82* and choose another answer.

A *V 6c*

Separating the papers on an item by item basis does take time, but it is time well spent. Return to page 77 and choose another answer.

B *V 8f 9*

This could very easily be put in multiple-choice form. Doing so would save the student time in answering the question and the teacher time in scoring it.

The short-answer question is another supply-type item. It is similar to the essay item in that the student must construct his own response but it is very dissimilar in the length of response. The essay item frequently requires many paragraphs or pages; the short-answer item typically can be answered with only a word or phrase. A short-answer test requires more time to prepare than an essay test but it also provides a wider sampling of behavior during a given test period. A one-hour short-answer test may contain as many as 60 or 70 items.

How does the efficiency of the short-answer item compare with that of the essay item?

a. The essay test is more efficient. (*P. 79A.*)

b. There is little difference. (*P. 85A.*)

c. The short-answer test is more efficient. (*P. 82B.*)

A *V 7c*

Alternative *1* is a much better question. Alternative *2* is too broad. It is so vague that a teacher might expect each of his students to interpret it somewhat differently. Each student is then answering a different question. The clever student will manipulate this type of vague question into one to which he knows the answer. Return to page *78* and do *d*.

B *V 10b 11*

Right! The short-answer and essay items place very different demands on the student. The essay item typically requires that the student use much more information in developing his answer. This in turn presents a much more serious problem in organization than with the short-answer item.

Short-answer questions do require the student to recall and produce an answer rather than recognize and choose it. This advantage may not be as great as it is sometimes assumed to be, however. There is, in fact, a substantial relationship between a student's ability to recognize a correct response from among alternatives (multiple-choice items) and his ability to recall it. If a student were put in a test situation he might not be able to recall as many facts as he could recognize. His relative position among his classmates, however, would be likely to remain relatively constant even if the item-type were shifted from recall to recognition.

Suppose two forms of a test were written, one with short-answer type items and the other with the same questions in a multiple-choice format. If both forms of this test were given to a group of students, what would you expect the results to show?

a. Students who did well on one form would also do well on the other. (*P. 83A.*)

b. There would be little relationship. (*P. 85B.*)

c. Students who did well on one form would do poorly on the other. (*P. 77A.*)

A *V 7f 8*

Number *2*, which requires the student to give the dates and a description of the last 4 amendments to the Constitution, could very easily be made into a series of multiple-choice questions or even more easily, into a matching question. Either of these two types is easier to score than an essay item.

Number *1*, while it could be put into multiple-choice form, is perhaps better as an essay item. Both *1* and *2* require recall, but what the student is required to recall is probably important enough to warrant these questions on a test.

Six more essay questions are given below. Read each question. Decide whether or not it is acceptable as it is. If not, decide why not. Then turn to the page indicated.

a. Discuss the Civil War. (*P. 77B.*)
b. List the four rules for clear writing given in your text. (*P. 78B.*)
c. In your opinion, what should be the government position in regard to farm price supports. (*P. 84B.*)
d. Compare the League of Nations with the United Nations. (*P. 86B.*)
e. How are a proton and a neutron similar? How are they different? (*P. 88B.*)
f. Why does acid turn litmus paper red? (*P. 80B.*)

B *V 9c 10*

You are right! The short-answer item is more efficient than the essay item. More questions can be asked in a given period of time and the student spends much less time writing out his answer.

The fact it is a more efficient item does not mean the short-answer item can or should replace the essay item in a testing program. Although the short-answer item is a supply-type item, the response the student is required to make is not very useful in measuring some of the skills and abilities which the essay item can tap. It is not very useful, for instance, in measuring a student's ability to organize material or compare and contrast alternative positions. It is also very difficult to write comprehension- or application-type items where the response expected is a single word or short phrase. Short-answer items are then largely restricted to questions which measure a student's ability to recall facts.

Short-answer items are useful for measuring the same types of objectives as essay items.

a. True. (*P. 79B.*)
b. False. (*P. 81B.*)

A *V 11a 12*

Good! The relationship is not a perfect one and may vary somewhat from one content area to another but, in general, a student's relative position on a test would not be expected to be markedly influenced by whether he had to produce or recognize the answers.

One problem associated with short-answer type items is the range of answers the students give. Many times these answers are more or less synonomous with the word the teacher wanted. He is then put in the position of having to decide which he will accept and which he will not. An even more difficult decision is involved when the question can be answered in more than one way, depending on how it is interpreted. Suppose a teacher writes the following question: "As a cyclone approaches, barometric pressure ______." The answer the teacher wants is "falls." He will probably accept "drops" or "goes down," but what about "fluctuates" or "changes"? Or suppose a teacher writes this item; "A dog is an example of a ______." The teacher wants "mammal" as the answer, but does not "living thing" also complete the sentence correctly? This may not be the answer the teacher has in his key, but it is correct.

The major problem encountered in scoring short-answer items is similar to that involved in scoring:

a. Essay items. (*P. 87B.*)

b. Multiple-choice items. (*P. 89A.*)

B *V 13a*

The blank is at the beginning of the sentence. The question could be easily rephrased to put the blank at the end. Return to page *87* and try *b*.

A *V 7d*

Essay items should measure important knowledge, skills, and discriminate among students. It is difficult to imagine very many courses where being able to name 5 insects would be an important instructional objective. In addition, if very much time had been spent studying insects this would probably be a very easy item which both good and poor students could answer. Question *1*, which requires the student to contrast insects and arachnids, is a much better question. Return to page *78* and do *e*.

B *V 8c*

The question asks for an opinion with which the teacher might agree or disagree but this hardly represents a valid basis for scoring the answer. In general, essay items should not ask for opinions but should require students to discuss, compose, compare, and contrast. Two exceptions would be when the teacher wants to know how clearly the student can express his opinion or how well he can defend it. If either of these were the case with question *c* it should be stated somewhat differently. Return to page *82* and do *d*.

A *V 9b*

In an essay item the student spends a considerable amount of time writing out his answer once he has decided what it is to be. The short-answer item does not require this. In addition, a student can answer 60 or 70 short-answer items in the time it takes to answer 4 or 5 essay items. Return to page *80* and choose another answer.

B *V 11b*

It might seem that recalling an answer is sufficiently different from recognizing one that there would be little relationship between them. This does not seem to be the case. In general, the student who does well on a test requiring recognition will also do well on one requiring recall. Return to page *81* and choose another answer.

A *V 7e*

Number *2* which asks the student to compare scoring problems on the essay and on completion items is a much better question than number *1* which asks him to list 3 rules. There is little reason to assume that the 3 rules given could not as easily have been 2 or 4 or 5. In addition, asking a student to write a list of 3 rules he has read does not seem to be measuring a very critical bit of knowledge. Return to page *78* and do *f*.

B *V 8d*

This question does not give the student much guidance. The comparison could be on the basis of development, representation, popularity, or any one of a number of other factors. It would be a better question if it were qualified by indicating which of these the teacher wanted to use as a basis for comparison. Return to page *82* and try *e*.

A *V 11c*

This is sometimes assumed to be true. The evidence suggests, however, that those who do well on recognition also tend to do well on recall. There is little evidence to suggest that the two are negatively related. Return to page *81* and choose another answer.

B *V 12a 13*

Right! In short-answer items the teacher must decide whether or not the answer the student produces is sufficiently close to the keyed answer to be scored as correct. This involves a considerable amount of subjectivity and reduces scoring reliability.

A teacher might decide to use short-answer type items despite the limited range of objectives which they are useful in measuring and the problems they present in scoring. If he does, the following guidelines should be observed: (1) Make sure the facts asked for are important. (2) Do not take sentences directly out of the book. (3) Have only one blank or require only one word or phrase as the answer. (4) If it is a fill-in-the-blank item, put the blank at the end of the sentence. (5) Be sure the question permits only one answer. (6) Be careful that the grammar of the sentence does not give it away.

Read each of the following short-answer items. Determine what, if anything, is wrong with each one and then turn to the page indicated to check your answer.

a. The ______ is the dense central part of an atom. (*P. 83B.*)
b. The standard of living is higher in ______ than it is in ______, but lack of ______ still hinders its development. (*P. 90A.*)
c. Jamestown was settled ______. (*P. 92A.*)
d. What is photosynthesis? (*P. 94A.*)
e. In the problem $23\overline{)426}$, the 23 is called the ______. (*P. 96A.*)
f. Where is the longest river in the world? (*P. 98A.*)
g. The quantity of electricity per unit of volume at a point in space is a definition of ______. (*P. 100A.*)
h. Who was the vice-president during Lincoln's first term as president? (*P. 89B.*)

A *V 7a*

The first item asks for opinion. If the teacher wants to determine how clearly a student can express his opinion this might be a good question. It might also be an acceptable means of determining the student's ability to support an opinion if it were stated somewhat differently. If it is meant only to elicit an opinion, however, it is not a good question because of scoring problems. It is easy to score opinions on the basis of the degree to which they coincide with those of the teacher. It is much more difficult to do so on the basis of right or wrong. The second question would be much easier to score objectively. Return to page *78* and do *b*.

B *V 8e*

This question requires the student to compare and contrast a proton and a neutron. Although it could be put in multiple-choice formation, it is an acceptable question as it is expressed here in essay form. Return to page *82* and do *f*.

C *V 17c*

This may be done in some cases, but not as a general rule. Return to page *91* and choose another answer.

A *V 12b*

Multiple-choice items require the student to choose the one best answer from among those given. He either chooses it or he does not and the item is scored accordingly. In short-answer items the student constructs his own answer and the teacher must then decide if that answer is close enough to the one he wants. Are these similar scoring problems? Return to page *83* and choose another answer.

B *V 13h 14*

There is nothing technically wrong with this item. Direct questions such as this one may have some advantage over fill-in-the-blank items for students who are young or who have had little experience in taking tests.

The point has been made that scoring is difficult and time-consuming when supply-type items are used. The questions can be written relatively quickly, however, Just the reverse is true of choice-type items. With choice-type items, particularly multiple-choice items, the teacher must spend a considerable amount of time writing the question but the items can be scored quickly and easily. Before beginning a discussion of particular choice-type items, we might do well to discuss some erroneous assumptions that are frequently made about such items. These assumptions often lead teachers to decide in favor of supply-type items when, in fact, choice-type items might serve their purpose better.

How do choice-type items compare with supply-type items?

a. They have many disadvantages and few advantages. (*P. 91A.*)

b. There are very few important advantages one way or the other. (*P. 93A.*)

c. They have some important advantages. (*P. 95A.*)

A *V 13b*

There are so many blanks and the sentence is so complex as to be virtually impossible to answer. Return to page *87* and try *c*.

B *V 15a*

It takes time and effort to write multiple-choice items that measure processes such as analysis but it can be done. Return to page *95* and choose another answer.

A *V 14a*

Although many teachers seem to feel this way, choice-type items, such as multiple-choice questions have many advantages over supply-type items for many testing purposes. Failure to recognize these advantages may lead a teacher to use an essay test when a multiple-choice test would have been as valid and more reliable and efficient. Return to page *89* and choose another answer.

B *V 16a 17*

Good! Item writing takes time and most of the disadvantages attributed to multiple-choice items can be overcome if more time and care is invested in writing them.

Time and care must, however, be supplemented with some "know-how" and although knowledge of a few principles of item writing will not assure success in writing multiple-choice tests, it will help. We will discuss these principles in three parts. The first covering general considerations, the second writing the stem or question, and the third writing the alternatives or choices. The first rule is to spread item writing out over a period of time rather than putting it off until the night before the test is given. This enables the teacher to spend more time writing items and also provides an opportunity for review and revision prior to the time the items are put on a test and given to the students. In general, the stem should be written first, then the correct response, and then the distractors (the incorrect responses). It is easier to revise items if each is put on a separate sheet or card. Five-by-eight index cards are excellent for this purpose.

Multiple-choice item construction typically begins with writing:

a. A question or incomplete statement. *(P. 93B.)*

b. A set of plausible incorrect responses to some questions. *(P. 97A.)*

c. A correct response the student is supposed to have learned. *(P. 88C.)*

A *V 13c*

There are many ways this question could be answered. An additional word or two would indicate to the student which of them the teacher wants. Return to page *87* and try *d*.

B *V 15b 16*

Fine! The ability to analyze a composition can be measured with multiple-choice items if the teacher is willing to spend the time and effort to write them. It will take a considerable amount of both, but this will be compensated for by increased ease and reliability of scoring the students' answers.

Another frequently made assumption is that multiple-choice items, by giving the student alternatives and requiring that he choose an answer from among them, is at best artificial and an oversimplification of the nature of knowledge, and at worst a violation of the student's right to use his own judgment in setting up an answer. In answer to the first, it should be pointed out that choosing among alternatives is as prevalent a fact of life as is creating responses. It should also be pointed out that although the response the student makes may be choosing an answer, the process by which he derives that answer may vary all the way from remembering to evaluating. It is a mistake to assume that all answers to all questions are equally correct so that one man's opinion is as valuable as another's. There are questions in which this is the case, but such questions do not belong on an achievement test. It is also commonly assumed that multiple-choice items must be made ambiguous so as to "cover up" the correct answer and that they encourage guessing. While a poorly-constructed test might be both ambiguous and encourage guessing, this again is a matter of items being poorly written rather than a necessary characteristic of multiple-choice items.

Most of the disadvantages attributed to multiple-choice items:

a. Can be overcome if more time and care is spent on item construction. *(P. 91B.)*

b. Are such that they must be recognized but are largely impossible to remedy. *(P. 94B.)*

A *V 14b*

Choice-type items differ from supply-type in the time it takes to write and score them. They also vary in reliability of performance and scoring, and economy in the use of teacher and student time. These are important differences. Return to page *89* and choose another answer.

B *V 17a 18*

Good! The first step in writing a multiple-choice item is typically the construction of the stem which is a question or incomplete statement.

There are a number of guidelines that should be observed in writing the stem of the item. It is important, first of all, that the stem indicate very clearly to the student what he is to answer. Direct questions are more likely to do this than are incomplete statements from which the student is to choose the alternative that best completes the statement. The stem should be stated as directly and concisely as possible, without lengthy qualifications. Whenever possible, the stem should pose a problem that is unique and requires something more than a one-word answer. Most of the items should require that the student do more than just recall what was said in class or read in a book.

Which of the following is the best stem for a multiple-choice item?

a. If a student computes a correlation coefficient and gets a value of 1.47 he should ______. *(P. 101A.)*

b. What should a student do if he computes a correlation coefficient and gets a value of 1.47? *(P. 97B.)*

c. Correlation coefficients are very useful in making predictions. What should a student do if he computes a correlation coefficient and gets a value of 1.47? *(P. 98B.)*

A *V 13d*

The answer to this question is too long to fit very comfortably into the short-answer category. The question should be rewritten so as to make it more specific or be expanded into an essay question. Return to page *87* and do *e*.

B *V 16b*

The assumptions that were discussed have developed because so many multiple-choice tests have been poorly-conceived and hurriedly written. It takes time and practice to write items which go beyond recall and recognition, but it can be done if the teacher is willing to invest the effort required. Return to page *92* and choose another answer.

A *V 14c*

Good! Choice-type items do have some important advantages over supply-type items.

The most versatile of the choice-type items is the multiple-choice item. The frames that follow, while applicable to choice-type items in general, are directed specifically to multiple-choice items. Among the most widely held misconceptions about multiple-choice items is that they cannot be used to measure the so-called higher mental processes and that they can only measure recognition and recall. As a matter of fact, multiple-choice items can be used to measure almost any measurable mental process. While many multiple-choice tests do measure no more than recognition and recall, the fault lies with the test builder not with the item type. A well-written multiple-choice item can measure comprehension and understanding as validly as any other type of test item can. It can also measure a student's ability to apply what he knows. Such items take much more time to write than do those that require only recall, but they can be written, and once written the students' answers can be scored quickly and reliably.

If a teacher wants to test for both recall of fact and ability to analyze a composition he can use multiple-choice items on part of the test but will almost surely have to use some other type of item to measure the ability to analyze a composition.

a. True. (*P. 90B.*)

b. False. (*P. 92B.*)

B *V 19b*

A specific determiner is a clue provided the student by the structure of the item. It is improbable that these types of clues would lower student scores. Return to page *97* and choose the other answer.

A *V 13e*

There is no serious error in this question. It could, however, be made into a multiple-choice question which would be easier to score. Return to page *87* and do *f*.

B *V 20a*

Alternative *1* was chosen by five students so it apparently has some degree of credibility. There is another alternative which seems to have had little attractiveness for the students. Return to page *99* and find it.

A *V 17b*

This is a necessary and important step in writing a multiple-choice item, but it is not generally the first one. Return to page *91* and choose another answer.

B *V 18b 19*

Good! This item asks a question which is direct and to the point with no extraneous words.

It is also important that the stem be grammatically correct both in how it is stated and how it leads into the alternatives. Care must be exercised that word usage in the stem does not give the answer away. Stating the stem in such a fashion that it clearly requires a plural response and having one plural and three singular answers among the alternatives, or ending a stem with "an" and having one answer which begins with a vowel and three which begin with consonants are two examples of how this can occur. Having the word or phrase which is the correct response appear somewhere in the stem is another example of a specific determiner.

What would be the effect of having many items with specific determiners on a test?

a. It would tend to raise scores. (*P. 99A.*)

b. It would tend to lower scores. (*P. 95B.*)

A *V 13f*

This question is not specific enough. Does the teacher want the countries through which it flows, the continent on which it is located, or the hemisphere in which it can be found? Return to page *87* and do *g*.

B *V 18c*

The first sentence does not really add anything to the stem. Return to page *93* and choose another answer.

A

V 19a 20

Correct! It would tend to raise scores, particularly those of the students who look for such clues on a test.

The task of writing the alternatives is made considerably easier if care is exercised to write a stem which has a defensibly correct answer and which allows for the writing of plausible distractors (incorrect responses). The correct response need not be absolutely correct or the only possible correct response. It must, however, be a better answer than any of the other alternatives. The alternatives should not permit the student to choose the correct one only on the basis of common sense or logic. Each should have some degree of attractiveness for the student who does not know what he must do to answer correctly. This is not tricking the student, it is testing whether he really understands or whether he has only a surface fact-level knowledge of a concept or principle.

In looking at the responses students made to a certain item a teacher notes that 5 of them chose alternative *1,* 14 choose alternative *2,* 7 choose alternative *3,* and 1 chose alternative *4.* Which of these alternatives does not seem to have one of the desirable characteristics of alternatives discussed above:

a. 1. (*P. 96B.*)

b. 3. (*P. 102A.*)

c. 4. (*P. 104A.*)

B

V 21a

In view of the other alternatives given, *A* does <u>not</u> seem to violate any of the suggestions on page *104*. Return to page *104*, reread the paragraph, and choose another answer.

A *V 13g*

This question is phrased in a very "bookish" fashion. It would be a better question and reward the rote learner less if it were rephrased. Return to page *87* and do *h*.

B *V 21b 22*

Good! Alternative *D* is qualified more than are the other three. If the teacher is not careful this may be true of many of the correct answers he writes. Without knowing what the stem is, there is no way to know for sure that *D* is the correct response, but as it stands it is the alternative that is most likely to violate one of the suggestions given on page *90*.

In addition to the general considerations already discussed there are a number of more specific guidelines that should be observed in writing the alternatives.

1. Whenever possible, write at least four alternatives.
2. Put the alternatives at the end of the stem. Do not insert them somewhere in the middle.
3. Arrange the alternatives in a vertical column, not across the page.
4. If there is a natural order among the alternatives (numerical or alphabetical), use it.
5. Make the alternatives as brief as possible by putting as much of the item as possible in the stem.

A teacher, in writing a multiple-choice item, arranged the alternatives in the following fashion:

a. 1934   b. 1812   c. 1776   d. 1860

On the basis of the guidelines provided above, which of the following statements is most accurate?

a. The arrangement of the alternatives is acceptable the way it stands. *(P. 103A.)*
b. The dates should be listed vertically instead of horizontally. *(P. 104B.)*
c. The dates should be put in a different order. *(P. 108A.)*
d. The dates should be listed vertically in a different order. *(P. 106A.)*

A *V 18a*

Although this is acceptable there is a better way of expressing this stem. Return to page *93* and find it.

B *V 23a 24*

Does it really make much difference what rule happened to have been discussed or presented second? This is a useless bit of information on which to base a test item.

Now try this one.

An essay item is:

A. Easy to prepare.
B. Good for measuring facts.
C. A choice-type item.
D. Easy for students to answer.

Turn to page *102B.*

A *V 20b*

Alternative *3* was chosen by 7 of the 26 students who took the test so it has some degree of attractiveness and must be a plausible possibility. There is a better answer to the question. Return to page *99* and find it.

B *V 24a 25*

There are two major weaknesses in this item. The stem does not provide enough orientation for the student and the alternatives are too heterogeneous.

Now try this one.

If a teacher wants to test a student's ability to organize material he should probably use an:

A. Multiple-choice item.
B. True-false item.
C. Completion item.
D. Essay item.

Turn to page *105*.

A

V 22a

Return to page *100*, check guidelines *3* and *4*, then choose another answer.

B

V 38b 29

Right! The most obvious shortcoming is the use of the word "never" but the item also is probably very much a fact, memory-type item.

Read each of the following items. Decide what, if anything, is wrong with them. Then turn to the page indicated.

a. If a teacher has had a course in educational psychology he is likely to be able to handle most problems that will arise in a classroom. (*P. 107B.*)

b. The first ten amendments to the Constitution are not called the Bill of Rights. (*P. 111B.*)

c. William Shakespeare was born in 1564, was the greatest English writer, and wrote nearly 400 plays. (*P. 114B.*)

d. Many African nations have low literacy rates. (*P. 112B.*)

e. Galileo's theory of relativity suggests that the mass of a body increases with its velocity. (*P. 121A.*)

f. All mammals feed their offspring with milk. (*P. 123B.*)

g. Wages should be based on amount of work done. (*P. 119A.*)

h. Three general rules must be observed when serving on a jury. (*P. 113B.*)

A *V 20c 21*

Good! An alternative chosen by only 1 student out of 26 is hardly an attractive one. For all practical purposes that alternative would not have to be included in the item.

Specific determiners can also be a serious problem among the alternatives. Among the most common are (1) correct response longer than the incorrect response, (2) correct response more familiar to the student than the incorrect response, and (3) correct response put in the same position in a number of questions. The correct response should not be more detailed or abstract than the other alternatives. If it is, it will tend to be longer and its length will give it away. All the alternatives should be equally familiar to the students. In fact, the distractors could be the correct answer to some question other than the one to that item. The correct response should be put in different positions among the alternatives.

The alternatives for a multiple-choice question are given below:

A. Recall.
B. Analysis.
C. Recognition.
D. Some types of applications.

Which of these alternatives is the least desirable?

a. Alternative *A.* (*P. 99B.*)
b. Alternative *D.* (*P. 100B.*)

B *V 22b*

You are half right! Return to page *100*, reread guideline *4*, and choose another answer.

A *V 25a 26*

The stem ends with "an," and the only response which begins with a vowel is the correct one.

Consider this one.

What is the best type of test item to use?

a. Multiple-choice.
b. True-false.
c. Completion.
d. Essay.

Turn to page *107A*.

B *V 38a*

Return to page *108* and look at suggestion *4*. Then reread the item and choose another answer.

A *V 22d 23*

Good! The dates should be put in an order from earliest to latest or vice versa and in a vertical column instead of across the page.

Now read this item and decide what, if anything, is wrong with it.

The second rule in writing essay items is to:

A. Base them on important objectives.
B. Write them very clearly.
C. Be sure they can be answered.
D. Be convinced that they discriminate.

To check your answer turn to page *101B*.

B *V 37a*

If the statement were false and he chose the alternative "The statement is probably true," how would you justify giving him one point? Return to page *111* and reread the material. Then choose another response.

A *V 26a 27*

There is no single best answer for this question. The teacher would find it difficult to defend which ever one he keyed as the correct one.

Now try this one.

Which of the following is not regarded by most experts, although there are some exceptions, as being measurable through the use of multiple-choice tests if they are skillfully written?

A. Recall.
B. Comprehension.
C. Application.
D. Evaluation.

Turn to page *109A*.

B *V 39a*

Common sense is likely to tell you there is no one course that can provide this kind of skill. Return to page *103* and do *b*.

A *V 22c*

You are half right. Return to page *100*, read guideline *3*, and choose another answer.

B *V 37c 38*

Good! He would lose one point.

The weightings given the choices when the item is true and when it is false are shown below.

	Weight of Statement	
	True	False
A. The statement is true.	+2	−2
B. The statement is probably true.	+1	−1
C. I do not know.	0	0
D. The statement is probably false.	−1	+1
E. The statement is false.	−2	+2

A number of other suggestions for writing better true-false items are given below:

1. Be sure the statements are related to important objectives.
2. Write the statements clearly and precisely and in such a fashion that more than recall is required to answer them.
3. Be sure the items require more than common sense and logic to answer.
4. Watch for words such as "never" and "all" which generally indicate false statements and "often" and "some" which generally indicate true statements.
5. Do not make false statements by writing or taking a true one and inserting the word "no" or "not."

Would you judge this true-false item to be a good or poor one on the basis of the suggestions given above?

"True-false items should never be used in the same test with essay items."

a. Good. (*P. 105B.*)

b. Poor. (*P. 103B.*)

A

V 27a 28

The question is very confusing with all the qualifications plus the negative. Consider this one?

In what year was the Battle of Waterloo fought?

a. 1815
b. 1776
c. 1865
d. 1563

Turn to page *110A*.

B

V 36b

There are many objectives that can be evaluated with either a true-false or multiple-choice item. In fact, many multiple-choice items could be broken up into three or four true-false items without changing the objective measured by the item. Return to page *116* and choose another answer.

A *V 28a 29*

This would be a better item if the dates were arranged in order.

Now try this one.

Which of the following was the best president?

A. Hoover.
B. Roosevelt.
C. Truman.
D. Eisenhower.

Turn to page *112A*.

B *V 40b*

How would you set up a matching item to test students' understanding of the causes of World War II? What types of things would they be expected to "match-up"? There is a better answer. Return to page *113* and find it.

A *V 36a 37*

Correct! There are many cases in which a multiple-choice item can be broken into three or four true-false items without changing the objective measured. Doing this, when appropriate, has the advantage of providing four scores (one for each true-false item) instead of the one that the multiple-choice item yields.

The problem of a high chance score, because there are only two choices on a true-false item, can be eased somewhat by requiring that the student not only choose true or false, but that he also indicate a degree of confidence in his choice. This can be done several ways. One method is to use a scale which forces the student to choose one of five alternatives:

A. The statement is true.
B. The statement is probably true.
C. I do not know.
D. The statement is probably false.
E. The statement is false.

If the statement is true and the student chooses alternative *A*, he gets two points. If he chooses *B*, he gets one point. If he chooses *C*, he gets no points. If he chooses *D*, he loses one point, and if he chooses *E*, he loses two points.

What would his score be if the statement were false and he were to choose alternative two?

a. He would get one point. (*P. 106B.*)
b. He would get no points. (*P. 113A.*)
c. He would lose one point. (*P. 108B.*)

B *V 39b*

This is no more than a true statement made false by inserting "not." This is not good item writing procedure. Return to page *103* and do *c*.

A

This item asks for an opinion. A teacher would be hard pressed to defend his choice of correct response.

How about this one?

H_2O:

A. Freezes at 32°C.
B. Has a light blue color.
C. Has a slight acid taste.
D. Is necessary to sustain life.

Turn to page *114A*.

B

The words "many" and "low" in this question are too vague. How many is "many"? Four? Ten? Fifteen? How low is "low"? 10 percent? 50 percent? 75 percent? Return to page *103* and try *e*.

A *V 37b*

The student gets no points only if he does not make a true or false choice. This student made a choice, a wrong one. Return to page *111* and choose another answer.

B *V 39h 40*

The number of rules is not really very important. What these rules are might be.

There is one other choice-type item that requires at least some mention. That is the matching item.

Matching items require students to match pairs of words or phrases. The matching may involve any of a variety of types of matches such as generals and battles, cities and states, symbols and words, or definitions. One major advantage of the matching item is its efficiency. The same set of words or phrases may yield as many as 10 or 12 student responses. This conserves student time in reading items and gives a large number of scorable responses during a test period. Major disadvantages of matching items are the limited range of objectives which they can measure and the difficulty of writing good matching exercises. It is very easy to spoil matching items through grammatical clues or poorly chosen or arranged sets of alternatives.

For which of the following would a matching item be most useful?

a. Testing a student's knowledge of the dates of the major sea battles of World War II. (*P. 115A.*)

b. Testing a student's understanding of the causes of World War II. (*P. 110B.*)

A *V 30a 31*

The item does not orient the student enough. No question is asked or implied.

Now try this one.

Dogs are not:

A. Mammals.
B. Invertebrates.
C. Warm-blooded.
D. Good pets.

Turn to page *123A*.

B *V 39c*

This item is a failure. It has three parts, one of which is true, one of which is false, and one of which may be true. It is likely to confuse rather than test the student. Return to page *103* and try *d*.

Correct! A matching item might be very useful in testing a student's knowledge of the dates of the major sea battles of World War II. There might be some question why he should be expected to learn them, but if he is it would fit very easily into a matching item.

In writing matching items the more homogeneous the two sets of items to be matched, the better the item is likely to be. In addition, at least one of the sets should be single words or very short phrases. There should be no more than 10 or 12 alternatives in any one set. A matching item in which there are more than 12 alternatives can be very confusing. The student must spend too much time trying to determine what the choices are and finding a particular one when he wants it. It is also useful to arrange the response alternatives in some order (e. g., alphabetical or chronological) to help the student find a response once he has decided which one he wants. It is generally advisable to have more response items than are required and the sets of items to be matched should be on the same page.

What is wrong with this matching item?

Zion	Idaho
Mitchell	Utah
Yosemite	North Carolina
Mt. Ranier	Ohio
Glacier	California
	Washington
	Minnesota

Turn to page *117A*.

There are two things wrong with this item. The first sentence in the stem adds nothing to the item and should be omitted, and the question could be reworded to get rid of the "not" in the second sentence.

Multiple-choice items are but one type of choice item. Another that has enjoyed wide popularity is the true-false item. True-false items are relatively easy to write and they provide an effective and efficient way of measuring what a student knows. They are, however, limited in the range of educational objectives they can be used to measure. They also allow for a high "guess-factor" since there are only two possible answers and they can very easily become fact-type items which measure only sheer recall. Despite these possible limitations, true-false items can, if carefully prepared, be used to measure some of the same objectives measured by multiple-choice items.

The question asked in many multiple-choice items could be put in a true-false format.

a. True. (*P. 111A.*)

b. False. (*P. 109B.*)

A *V 41a 42*

Three of the items in the first column are national parks and two of them are mountains. It would be better if the first column were all mountains or all national parks.

What is wrong with this matching item?

Hop Frog	Will James
The Bishop's Silver	Wallace Stegner
Midnight	Edgar Allen Poe
Fourth of July	Victor Hugo

Turn to page *119B*.

B *V 39d*

The terms "many" and "low" are ambiguous and make the question difficult to interpret. How many is many? Five? Ten? Fifteen? How low is low? 10 percent? 25 percent? 50 percent? Return to page *103* and try *e*.

This item asks for personal opinion.

How about this one?

How does the author of your text define high reliability?

A. Greater than .30.
B. Greater than .50.
C. Greater than .70.
D. Greater than .90.

Turn to page *120A*.

A *V 39g*

It would probably be difficult to find a consensus of opinion among experts on this item. How then is the teacher going to score it? Return to page *103* and try *h*.

B *V 42a 43*

The number of alternatives is the same in both columns. If the student knows three he gets the fourth by elimination. It would be better if an author or two were added to the second column.

Now try this one.

Amphibians emerge, fish increase	Mountains of Canada and White Mountains rise
No land life, lack of fossil record	Mountain rise in western U. S.
Primitive man, elephants in North America	Columbia Plateau rises, North America and Asia joined
Horse goes to Asia, era of grazing animals	Much volcanic activity, iron formed
	Coal found in North America and Asia

Turn to page *121B*.

How one author defines high reliability is hardly worth a test item. Other authors might define it very differently.

Now try this one.

Psychology is the study of animal and human:

A. Behavior.
B. Conscious experience.
C. People.
D. Unconscious states.

Turn to page *122A*.

A *V 39e*

The substance of the statement is true except that it is Einstein's not Galileo's theory of relativity. Making a true statement false by this type of substitution is not good item writing practice. Return to page *103* and try *f*.

B *V 43a*

This would be a very difficult item because of the complexity of the alternatives. It could be improved by rewriting or restructuring one of the columns.

Turn to page *125*.

The stem has a specific determiner. No student is likely to choose people as an answer with the stem written as it is.

Now try this last one.

Teachers often have difficulty motivating students. Which of the following terms is not used in relationship to motivation?

A. Need.
B. Drive.
C. Cue.
D. Goal.

Turn to page *116A*.

A *V 31a 32*

The "not" is confusing and the alternatives are not homogeneous. "Good pets" does not seem to belong.

How about this one?

Which of the following do you consider most important in test construction?

A. Convenience.
B. Economy.
C. Reliability.
D. Validity.

Turn to page *118A*.

B *V 39f*

This is an acceptable item as it is written. The "all" is not a specific determiner here because the statement is true. Because "all" is so often associated with false statements, however, it must be used carefully or can provide a very useful clue to the clever test-taker. Return to page *103* and read *g*.

CHAPTER 6

Administering and Scoring the Test

A *VI 1*

The validity and reliability of even the best set of items can be drastically reduced if the test is not administered and scored properly. Proper administration begins with providing the students ample time to prepare for a test. "Snap quizzes" can serve some rather limited objectives but, in general, students should be notified well in advance of any test. The announcement of a test should include not only the date but also give some indication of the number and types of items to be used and how heavily the test is to be weighted in determining final marks. The teacher should also specify what areas of content are to be covered. This type of information serves two important functions. First of all, it gives the student some guidance in his studying. If the teacher writes valid tests, they can have a direct positive influence on his student's study habits. Telling the students what type of test to expect before the test provides guidance when it is likely to do the most good. This type of information also can serve to reduce student anxiety about the test. A little anxiety might facilitate performance on a test but some students suffer so much anxiety about tests that it interferes with their performance. Adequate warning and preparation can help reduce their test anxiety.

Three teachers make the following announcements in class. Which is inconsistent with what you have just read?

a. "We will have the final test on this unit the day after tomorrow." (*P. 126A.*)

b. "Your test on this unit will consist of 40 multiple-choice and 20 true-false items." (*P. 128A.*)

c. "The text will cover pages 324 through 507 in your book plus your class notes." (*P. 130A.*)

B *VI 2a*

It is generally better testing procedure to provide each student with his own set of test questions. The reading problem can be minimized by careful attention to the organization and reading level of the questions.

Return to page *126* and choose another answer.

A

VI 1a 2

Right! Two days is not enough warning to give for a unit test.

One or two days before the test is to be given the teacher might well go through specific directions for the test. This provides some additional last-minute information for the student and also saves time on the test day. The day of the test each student should be provided with his own set of the questions. If proper attention has been given to writing the directions and the test has been carefully reproduced, there should be few questions about it. If questions are raised during the test period they should be answered, but questioning should not be encouraged. A constant procession of student questions is very distracting. It is also a good idea to put the time remaining in the test period on the chalkboard periodically. This helps those students who do not have watches and is a reminder to all the students that the test does have a time limit.

It is good testing procedure to read the questions aloud rather than have each student have to read them himself from his own test booklet.

a. True. (*P. 125B.*)

b. False. (*P. 128B.*)

B

VI 3a

If students feel a test is invalid we might think they would refuse to take it seriously enough to cheat. This does not seem to be the case. Return to page *128* and choose another answer.

A *VI 4a*

Cheating must be treated as a serious offense regardless of how common it might be. Its incidence should not influence how severely we judge it. Return to page *130* and choose another answer.

B *VI 5a*

Neither weighting nor correction for guessing is likely to have a dramatic effect on validity. Return to page *129* and choose another answer.

A *VI 1b*

This indicates to the student what type of items he can expect. It is good testing practice to provide students with this kind of information. Return to page *125* and choose another answer.

B *VI 2b 3*

Good! Each student should have his own set of questions. The reading problem can be solved for all except the very young or very poor reader by keeping the reading level of the questions well below the grade level at which the test is given.

Among the more persistent problems encountered in testing is that of cheating. Cheating comes in many forms, from sneaking a copy of a test before it is given to sidelong glances at someone else's paper during the test period. There is no way to prevent all cheating, but there are some practices which can reduce it. Test security must be maintained carefully while the test is being prepared, when it is being reproduced, and where it is stored. The test should be administered in an orderly fashion with a minimum of confusion which could provide a cover for cheating. If possible seating should be arranged to reduce the possibility of copying. Two forms of the test with the items in different orders is effective in reducing copying. As important as any of these procedures, however, is the quality of the examination. If the students view the test as unimportant and unfair they are much more prone to cheat than if they view it as an important and valid measure of their achievement.

What effect is the students' doubting the validity of a test likely to have on cheating?

a. Reduce it. (*P. 126B.*)

b. Increase it. (*P. 130B.*)

c. Have no effect. (*P. 132A.*)

A *VI 4b 5*

Correct! The fact it is so common should not influence how severely we punish cheating.

Teachers are often tempted, when scoring tests, to weight items differently. If one question measures a skill or ability that seems more important than another this appears to be a very logical thing to do. Despite how logical it appears on the surface it is seldom worth the time it takes. Weighting rarely has any appreciable effect on either reliability or validity. The same is true of correcting for guessing. There are a number of formulas which have been developed to correct for guessing. None of them is likely to be worth the added work it requires when scoring.

Which of the following is most true of weighting items and correcting for guessing?

a. They increase validity to such a degree as to be worth the time they take. (*P. 127B.*)

b. They increase reliability to such a degree as to be worth the time they take. (*P. 131A.*)

c. They do not increase either reliability or validity enough to be worth the time they take. (*P. 132B.*)

B *VI 6a*

Three students had a score of 4. Return to page *132,* find the score of 6, and check the number of students who had that score.

A *VI 1c*

Students should know exactly what is to be covered on a test. Return to page *125* and choose another answer.

B *VI 3b 4*

Right! Doubt about the validity of a test increases the probability students' will cheat.

It is sometimes assumed that there is less likelihood of cheating on an essay test than on a multiple-choice test. This may be true to some degree, but item type probably has a greater impact on how the students cheat than on how much they cheat. Copying answers is somewhat easier on a multiple-choice test, while "crib sheets" are likely to be somewhat more useful in an essay test. Regardless of how the cheating is done, however, it is a serious offense and should be dealt with accordingly. Failure of the test is not too harsh a punishment for cheating. If the test is a very critical one a penalty as severe as failure in the course may be warranted.

Because it is so widespread, teachers must be careful not to punish cheating too severely.

a. True. (*P. 127A.*)

b. False. (*P. 129A.*)

A *VI 5b*

Neither weighting nor correcting for guessing is likely to have a dramatic effect on reliability. Return to page *129* and choose another answer.

B *VI 6b*

Six is the score. Return to page *132*, and find 6 in the score column, and check on how many students received that score.

A

VI 3c

Students' doubts about the validity of a test do have an influence on cheating. Return to page *128*, reread the paragraph, and choose another answer.

B

VI 5c 6

Good! Neither weighting nor correcting for guessing is likely to have a dramatic effect on either validity or reliability.

The number of points a student receives on a test is referred to as his "raw score." By itself this raw score means very little. One way to give it meaning is to put it in relationship to the raw scores attained by other students on the same test. The easiest way to do this is in a frequency distribution which shows how many students received each score. An example of a frequency distribution is given below.

SCORE	NUMBER OF STUDENTS
9	2
8	4
7	5
6	9
5	7
4	3
3	4

The top score of 9 was achieved by 2 students. Four students had the bottom score of 3.

How many students had a score of 6?

a. 3. (*P. 129B.*)

b. 6. (*P. 131B.*)

c. 9. (*P. 134A.*)

A

Correct! The range is 7 points (40-33) and the distribution is skewed. (It piles up at the upper end.)

It is frequently useful to know what the average score is in a distribution. Among the types of average scores most useful to the teacher are the <u>mean</u> and <u>median</u>. To find the mean of a set of scores you add them all together and divide by the total number of scores involved. If 4 students receive scores of 7, 4, 3, and 6 the mean of these scores is 5 (7 + 4 + 3 + 6 = 20, 20/4 = 5).

What is the mean of the following distribution of scores?

SCORE	FREQUENCY
6	2
5	2
4	4
3	1
2	1

a. 4.3. (*P. 135A.*)

b. 2.0. (*P. 137A.*)

c. 1.0. (*P. 139A.*)

B

The median is the middle score. Is 47 the middle score in this set of scores? Return to page *135* and choose another answer.

A

Right! Nine students receive a score of 6.

Two important characteristics of a distribution are its range and shape. The range is determined by subtracting the bottom score from the top score. The shape can be determined by inspection. If the number of students is approximately the same at each score value the distribution is said to be flat. If the scores "pile up" at one end or the other the distribution is said to be skewed. Generally score frequencies become smaller at the ends and pile up in the middle. Such a distribution is often referred to as bell-shaped.

A frequency distribution is given below.

SCORE	FREQUENCY
40	9
39	8
38	9
37	6
36	3
35	2
34	1
33	1

What is the range and shape of this distribution?

a. It is skewed with a range of 7 points. (*P. 133A.*)

b. It is skewed with a range of 9 points. (*P. 136A.*)

c. It is bell-shaped with a range of 7 points. (*P. 138A.*)

B

Percentile rank refers to the percentage of students who scored below a given score value. It does not refer to percentage correct on a test. Return to page *138* and choose another answer.

A

VI 8a 9

Right! You have multiplied each score value times its frequency (6 X 2 = 12, 5 X 2 = 10, 4 X 4 = 16, 3 X 1 = 3 and 2 X 1 = 2) and divided the sum of these values by the total number in the distribution (2 + 2 + 4 + 1 + 1 = 10).

The median is the middle score in a distribution. It is found by dividing the total number of scores by two and finding which score is at that point. For instance, the median of the distribution 9, 7, 6, 6, 4, 3, 3, 3, 1, is 4. There are 9 scores and 4 is the middle score.

What is the median of the following set of scores?

47, 46, 44, 40, 37, 37, 35, 34, 33, 32, 31, 30, 24

a. 47. (*P. 133B.*)

b. 37. (*P. 136B.*)

c. 35. (*P. 138B.*)

B

VI 11a

There are 14 students who scored less than 13 and 13 is 56 percent of 25. You have forgotten that you take all these below a score value plus one-half of those at that score when determining percentile ranks. That means 14 + one-half of 5 (the number of students who scored 13). Return to page *137* and choose another answer.

A *VI 7b*

The top score is 40; the bottom score is 33. Is this a range of 9 points? Return to page *134* and choose another answer.

B *VI 9b*

Is 37 the middle score in this set of scores? Return to page *135*, recount the scores, and choose another answer.

A *VI 8b*

What you have done is add column 1 and divide by the number of students. What you forgot was that *2* students had scores of 6, *2* had scores of 5, *4* had scores of 4, etc. You must multiply each score by its frequency and add these values. Return to page *133*, rework the problem, and choose another answer.

B *VI 10b 11*

Correct! Percentile rank refers to the percentage of students who scored below a given score value.

Percentile ranks are not difficult to compute by hand. The procedure is outlined below:

A. Set up a frequency distribution.

B. Add a cumulative frequency column which indicates the total number of students who scored at or below each score value.

C. Determine percentile ranks by dividing the total number of scores below plus one-half those at each score value by the total number of scores.

An example is given below:

SCORE	FREQUENCY	CUMULATIVE FREQUENCY	PERCENTILE RANK
16	1	25	98
15	3	24	90
14	2	21	80
13	5	19	
12	6	14	44
11	4	8	24
10	3	4	10
9	0	1	4
8	1	1	2
7	0	0	0

All the percentile ranks have been filled in except for the raw score of 13. What is the percentile rank of a raw score of 13?

a. 56. (*P. 135B.*)
b. 66. (*P. 139B.*)
c. 76. (*P. 140A.*)

A *VI 7c*

There were 9 students with a score of 40, 8 with a score of 39, 9 with a score of 38, 6 with 37, 3 with 36, 2 with 35, 1 with 34, and 1 with 33. Do these scores pile up in the middle? Return to page *134* and choose another answer.

B *VI 9c 10*

Good! There are 13 scores. The 7th, or middle score, is 35.

The point has been made that tests cannot be used to indicate precisely how much a student knows. They can only indicate where he stands relative to others who took the same test. It would be very useful then to be able to convert a student's raw score into some value which indicates relative standing. Rank ordering does this, but the significance of a rank order depends in part on how many there are in the group being ordered. Being 5th in a group of 500 is very different from being 5th in a group of 5. What is needed is some value which takes into account not only rank order but also the number in the group. The percentile rank is defined as the percentage of scores which lie below a given score value. If a score value has a percentile rank of 80 this means that 80 percent of the scores in the distribution lie below that score value.

A score value of 72 in a test has a percentile rank of 37. If a student gets a score of 72 on this test it means:

a. He has answered 37 percent of the items on the test correctly. (*P. 134B.*)

b. He has done better than 37 percent of the students who took the test. (*P. 137B.*)

A

VI 8c

What you have done is add up the frequency column and divide by 10. This column indicates only how many students received each of the score values. If you want the total of all the scores you must multiply each frequency by its appropriate score value and add up these figures (6 X 2 = 12, 5 X 2 = 10, 4 X 4 = 16, 3 X 1 = 3, 2 X 1 = 2 and 12 + 10 + 16 + 3 + 2 = 43). Return to page *133*, reread the problem, and choose another answer.

B

VI 11b 12

Good! Fourteen (the number of students who scored less than 13) plus one-half of 5 (the number who scored 13) is 16.5. 16.5 is 66 percent of 25 so the percentile rank of a score of 13 is 66.

Another distribution is given below:

SCORE	FREQUENCY	CUMULATIVE FREQUENCY	PERCENTILE RANK
9	2	10	90
8	1	8	75
7	3	7	65
6	2	4	
5	2	2	10

What is the percentile rank of a score of 6?

a. 30. *(P. 140B.)*

b. 40. *(P. 141A.)*

c. 50. *(P. 144A.)*

A

VI 11c

There were 19 students who scored at or below 13 and 19 is 76 percent of 25. When determining the percentile rank of a score, however, you use all those below plus one-half of those at the score value. This means 14 (the number who scored less than 13) plus one-half of 5 (the number who scored 13) is what you should have used. Return to page *137*, rework the problem, and choose another answer.

B

VI 12a 13

Right! There were 2 who scored less than 6. When these 2 are added to one-half of those who scored 6 and this is divided by the total number in the distribution, the percentile rank of a score of 6 is 30.

A frequency table is given below.

SCORE	FREQUENCY
5	1
4	3
3	7
2	4
1	3
0	2

What is the percentile rank of a score of 4?

a. 95. *(P. 142A.)*

b. 87.5. *(P. 144A.)*

c. 64.5. *(P. 145A.)*

Whoops! Four students scored at or below 6. Percentile rank is based on all those below but only one-half those at the score value involved. Return to page *139* and choose another answer.

A

You have taken all these below 4 plus <u>all</u> those at 4 to determine the percentile rank. You should take only one-half those at the score value involved. Return to page *140* and choose another answer.

A

How did you get 50? Percentile rank is determined by taking the number who are below a given score value (in this case 2 since there were 2 students who scored fewer than 6 points) plus one-half of those at that score value (in this case one-half of 2 because these were 2 students who scored 6 points). This value is divided by the total number of students in the distribution. There are 10 students in the distribution so this means 2 + 1/2 (2) or 2 + 1 divided by 10. Return to page *139* and choose the correct answer.

Correct! The score value of 4 has a percentile rank of 87.5.

Percentile ranks are among the most useful items of information a student can be given about his performance on a test. In fact, teachers might be well-advised to provide students with their percentile ranks on every test they take. It is generally not good practice, however, to add percentile ranks in determining final grades. It is better to add up the raw scores in the tests that have been given and make up a new set of percentile ranks based on these composites of raw scores.

Turn to page *147*.

To determine the percentile rank of a given score value you take <u>all</u> those below plus one-half of those at that score value and divide this by the total number of students in the distribution. Return to page *140*, do it this way, and choose another answer.

CHAPTER 7

Analyzing and Revising the Items

A

VII 1

An important part of testing is the analysis and revision of items to improve their functioning in a test. Since a discriminatory test is designed to "spread students out," it is important that the items used discriminate between good and poor students. They should be written so that students who have met the objectives of the course have a higher probability of answering them than those who have not. Among the most important factors influencing discrimination is the difficulty level of the item. An item which is so easy that everyone gets it right is of no use in separating good students from poor ones. Neither is an item which is so difficult that no one gets it right.

What kinds of items would discriminate among the students in the upper 10 percent of the class?

a. Easy items. (*P. 148A.*)

b. Items of intermediate difficulty. (*P. 150A.*)

c. Difficult items. (*P. 152A.*)

B

VII 2a

The alternatives chosen are shown along the top. The number of students choosing each is shown in the body of the table. Five of the 20 chose alternative *a*. The question is how many chose alternative *b*? Return to page *152* and choose another answer.

A *VII 1a*

The students in the upper 10 percent would all be likely to get the easy items correct. Would this spread them out? Return to page *147* and choose another answer.

B *VII 3a*

Whoops! 20 percent of the upper group had the item correct but the difficulty index is based on the upper and lower groups combined. Return to page *154* and choose another answer.

A *VII 2b*

You are looking in the row which shows the choices of the upper 27 percent. The question asks about the lower 27 percent. Return to page *152* and choose another answer.

B *VII 4b*

There were 20 in the lower group who chose alternative *a*. The question asks for the difference between the lower and upper groups in choosing alternative *a*. Return to page *151* and choose another answer.

A *VII 1b*

Most of the students in the upper 10 percent of the class would be likely to answer items of intermediate difficulty correctly. These items might spread them out some but probably not much. Return to page *147* and choose a better answer.

B *VII 4a*

Fine! There were 30 in the upper group and 20 in the lower who chose the correct alternative. The difference then is 10.

This difference of 10 now must be related to the number of students involved. The maximum difference possible would occur if every student in the upper group chose the correct alternative and none in the lower group did. In the example we have just been working with, it would occur if all 50 of those in the upper group chose the correct alternative and none in the lower group did. If there are 20 in each group, this value would be 20; if there are 125 in each group, it would be 125.

If there are 35 in the upper and 35 in the lower group, what is the maximum difference possible in an item analysis table?

a. 0. *(P. 154B.)*

b. 35. *(P. 153B.)*

c. 70. *(P. 156A.)*

A

Correct! Two students in the upper and 4 in the lower group chose alternative *a*. That means that 6 of 20 or 30 percent chose it. If that is the correct response, the difficulty index for the item is 30 percent. It should be noted that as difficulty goes up this index goes down and vice versa.

Discrimination refers to the degree to which good students answer correctly and poor students do not. Using the table we have been employing (p. 153), this would be reflected in the difference between the number of students in the upper and lower groups who chose the correct response. In the preceding table, for instance, 5 students in the upper and 3 in the lower group chose alternative *c*. If that is the correct response, the discrimination of the item is reflected in the difference between these two values. The difference of 2, however, would be more significant if there were only 5 students in each group than if there were 500. The index of discrimination then must take into account not only the difference between the numbers of students in the two groups who chose correctly, but also the total number of students involved.

An item analysis table is shown below.

	ALTERNATIVE				
	a	b	c	d	
Upper 27%	30	5	5	10	50
Lower 27%	20	10	15	5	50

If alternative *a* is the correct response, how many more students in the upper than in the lower group chose correctly?

a. 10. (*P. 150B.*)

b. 20. (*P. 149B.*)

c. 30. (*P. 153A.*)

B

This is the difficulty of the item. (Thirty-six of 80 chose correctly.) Go back to page *153* and determine the discrimination.

A

VII 2

Right! It would be the difficult items which would be most likely to spread the brighter students out. They would be likely to get most of the others correct.

It is possible to set up a table which can provide data on both difficulty and discrimination. The first step in setting up the table is to define good and poor students relative to the content and objectives of the test. The most convenient and available measure is the total score on the test being analyzed. The students in the upper 27 percent and lower 27 percent should be used as the good and poor groups. These percentages can be varied if the class is very large or very small, but for reasons we will not discuss here, 27 percent should be used whenever possible. Once these groups have been established the number of times each alternative was chosen in each of the two groups can be put in a table that looks like this:

	ALTERNATIVES				
	a	b	c	d	
Upper 27%	3	7	5	5	20
Lower 27%	5	8	4	3	20
	8	15	9	8	

This table indicates that of the 20 students in the upper 27 percent of the class, 3 chose alternative *a*, 7 chose alternative *b*, 5 chose alternative *c*, and 5 chose alternative *d*.

How many of the 20 students in the lower 27 percent chose alternative *b*?

a. 5. (*P. 147B.*)

b. 7. (*P. 149A.*)

c. 8. (*P. 154A.*)

B

VII 3c

Forty percent of the lower group chose alternative *a*, but the difficulty index is based on both the upper and lower groups. Return to page *154* and choose another answer.

A

VII 4c

There were 30 in the upper group who chose alternative *a*. The question asks for the difference between the lower and upper groups in number choosing that alternative. Return to page *151* and choose another answer.

B

VII 5b 6

Right! With 35 in each group the maximum difference between the number of correct choices in the two groups would be 35. This would occur only if all those in the upper group chose the correct alternative and none in the lower group did.

We will use the following item analysis table to illustrate exactly how the discrimination index is computed.

	ALTERNATIVES				
	a	b	c	d	
Upper 27%	15	45	20	20	100
Lower 27%	25	20	25	30	100

First of all, for purposes of review, what is the difficulty level of the item if *b* is the correct alternative? You should have answered 32.5 percent because 65 of the 200 students chose alternative *b*. The first step in determining discrimination from this table is to find the difference between the number of students in the upper and lower groups who chose the correct alternative. For this item, 45 in the upper group and 20 in the lower group chose alternative *b*. The difference then is 25. Because there are 100 students in each group the maximum possible difference would be 100 and the ratio of the observed difference (25) to the maximum possible difference (100) is 25/100. Expressed in decimal form this becomes .25.

If alternative *d* is the correct response, what is the discrimination of the item upon which the following table is based?

	ALTERNATIVES			
	a	b	c	d
Upper 27%	0	1	13	26
Lower 27%	2	8	20	10

a. .40 (*P. 155A.*)
b. .45 (*P. 151B.*)

A

Good! Eight of the 20 students in the lower 27 percent on the test chose alternative *b*.

A table, such as the one shown in the preceding frame, can be prepared for each item. If a five-by-eight index card is used, the item itself can be put on the back of the card or on one-half of the card with the table on the other half. Because an item may be used and analyzed a number of time, it is advisable to allow room for recording a number of analyses on the same card. Once the table has been prepared, discrimination and difficulty indices are easily established. Below is an example of another item analysis table.

ALTERNATIVES

	a	b	c	d	
Upper 27%	2	1	5	2	10
Lower 27%	4	2	3	1	10

There are 10 students in the upper 27 percent group and 10 in the lower 27 percent group. Let us assume that alternative *c* was the correct response. Eight of the students in the two groups (5 in the upper and 3 in the lower) chose the correct alternative. Using the percentage correct as the index of difficulty, this item has a difficulty of 40 percent (40 percent of the students in these 2 groups gave the correct answer).

What would be the difficulty level if alternative *a* were the correct response?

a. 20 percent. (*P. 148B.*)

b. 30 percent. (*P. 151A.*)

c. 40 percent. (*P. 152B.*)

B

If equal numbers in the upper and lower groups choose the correct alternative the discrimination difference would be 0. That is not the maximum difference possible. Return to page *150* and choose another answer.

Correct! 26-10=16. Since there are 40 in each group, the maximum possible difference is 40. The discrimination then is 16/40 or .40.

The item has difficulty level of 45 percent which makes it a relatively difficult item but its discrimination index of .40 is adequate. It is good rule of thumb to try to write items of about 50 percent difficulty with discriminations above .25. On this particular item no one in the upper group and only one person in the lower group chose alternative *a.* This would be a good place to start revising this item. Alternative *c* was the choice of 13 students in the upper group and 20 in the lower group. It may be an excellent incorrect alternative, but its attractiveness may also be due to ambiguities in the item so it should be checked over.

The numbers of students in the upper and lower 27 percent of a class choosing each of the four alternatives to a multiple choice test are given below. Arrange them in an item analysis table, determine difficulty and discrimination and indicate where you would start in revising the item. The correct alternative is *c*.

	Upper 27%	Lower 27%
a	2	8
b	0	0
c	20	8
d	3	9

The answers are on page *156B.*

A *VII 5c*

If there were only 35 in each group it would be impossible to have a difference of 70 between them. Return to page *150* and choose another answer.

B *VII 7a*

	ALTERNATIVES			
	a	b	c	d
Upper 27%	2	0	20	3
Lower 27%	8	0	8	9

Difficulty 56 percent.

Discrimination .48

Revision would probably start with alternative *b*, which was chosen by no one in either group.

Go on to page *159A*.

CHAPTER 8

Assigning Marks

A

VIII 1

After the classroom test has been written, administered, and scored the teacher faces the problem of assigning marks. Basically marks are symbols used to rate achievement. They may be letters (*A, B, C, D, F*) numerals (*1, 2, 3, 4, 5, 6*), or words (*high, average, low*). Marks serve a number of purposes. They provide those who are concerned with information about how well a student is doing. They can be used to help the student make educational and/or vocational plans for the future, and they can be used to motivate student behavior.

Marks serve no useful purpose; since teachers must assign them they should know something about the best procedures for doing so.

a. True. (*P. 160A.*)
b. False. (*P. 162A.*)

B

VIII 2a 3

Good! If based on carefully devised techniques, the relationship between marks and achievement should be a very close one.

In making decisions about marks there are numbers of questions that must be answered. One of them we have already discussed to some extent in the context of testing. That is whether or not marks should be assumed to reflect some absolute level of achievement or a level relative to classmates. Percentage scores have been widely used and often assumed to reflect some percentage of total mastery. The problem is defining what constitutes mastery and setting up some sort of scale that indicates what percentage of mastery a student has achieved. Because of this difficulty most marking should probably be done in terms of relative achievement with the student's classmates forming the "norm group." A problem with this is that classes may vary widely in ability so a student who is at the top of one class may not have achieved as much as a student in the middle of another class. The obvious way out of this dilemma is to adjust the grades assigned to the ability level of the class, giving more *A's* in a high ability class than in a lower ability class. The structure should not be set in such a fashion, however, that outstanding work in a low ability class cannot be rewarded with an *A*. There is little justification for denying the possibility of an *A* to a student just because he happens to be in a low ability class.

Is marking on the curve absolute or relative marking?

a. Absolute. (*P. 160B.*)
b. Relative. (*P. 163A.*)

A *VIII 1a*

Marks can serve a number of useful purposes if they are assigned carefully. Return to page *159* and choose another answer.

B *VIII 3a*

It is absolute in the sense that the numbers of students who are to receive each mark is set, but in the way the words relative and absolute are used on page *159*, it is not. What mark a student is assigned depends on his relative standing in the group. Return to page *159* and choose another answer.

A *VIII 2b*

Too often it is only a moderate one, but it can be much more than that if time and effort is expended to develop valid and reliable techniques to use as a basis for assigning marks. Return to page *162* and choose another answer.

B *VIII 4a*

The problem associated with the use of gain scores are many and difficult. Because they are so difficult to resolve, gain scores should be used sparingly and carefully. Return to page *163* and choose another answer.

A *VIII 1b 2*

Good! The statement is false. Marks can serve a number of useful purposes. Teachers must, however, know something about marks and marking systems to capitalize on their usefulness.

It is often charged that marks do not accurately reflect what a student knows or has learned and as a matter of fact often get in the way of learning. This may well be the case if the mark is assigned on the basis of poorly defined objectives and hurriedly written tests or unreliable observations. When this occurs there may be a considerable discrepancy between what a student learns or knows and the mark he receives. The fault, however, lies with the way the marks were assigned not with the assignment of marks as such.

Which of the following statements about the relationship between marks and achievement is most accurate?

a. It can and should be a very close one. (*P. 159B.*)

b. It can be at best only a moderate one. (*P. 161A.*)

B *VIII 5a*

The student's ability and attitude are frequently considered when marks are entered on a report card. As soon as this occurs the mark is not just a report of measurement but also reflects judgment. Return to page *164* and choose another answer.

A

VIII 3b 4

Correct! In marking on the curve the number of students who are to receive each mark may be set, but what mark a student receives depends on his relative position in the class.

Another question that arises in marking is whether the marks should be assigned on the basis of improvement or on the basis of status. In using improvement as the criterion, the teacher collects information about the student prior to the beginning of instruction and uses this as the basis for determining growth. There are a number of problems associated with growth measures. Two technical problems are the difficulty of developing good pre- and post-measures of achievement and the low reliability of gain scores. Another problem is whether gain can be made to be viewed by students as being as important a measure of success as status. In theory it seems feasible; in practice it may not be.

In most instances grades should be based on:

a. Gain. (*P. 161B.*)

b. Status. (*P. 164A.*)

B

VIII 6a

These marks do reflect measurement because they are based, at least partially, on scores on tests and papers. They reflect more than just measurement, however. Return to page *166* and choose another answer.

A

Right! There are so many problems associated with gain scores that marks should, in most cases, be based on status rather than gain.

A third question that must be considered is whether marks should report only the results of measurement or whether they should reflect both measurement and judgment. Measurement refers to assigning numerals to objects according to certain rules. The number of items a student gets correct on a test is a measurement. If the test is carefully developed and administered, this measurement may be very precise and objective and could be used as the sole basis for assigning marks. Frequently, however, marks are based not only on the results of measurement but also reflect the teacher's judgment of how good a score is. This judgment tends to be highly subjective. One person may judge a score as a good score while another person may judge it a poor one. It is also often very imprecise. What a teacher means when he says this is that a good score is often difficult to determine.

The marks teachers put on report cards are generally no more than a teacher's report of the results of certain measurements taken during a six- or nine-week period.

a. True. (*P. 162B.*)

b. False. (*P. 166A.*)

B

These marks do reflect judgment because the teacher's opinion of the students' attitudes influences the mark assigned. The mark is also, however, based partially on the scores received on tests and papers. Return to page *166* and choose another answer.

A *VIII 7a*

Teacher judgments are often subjective and imprecise. Would adding such a factor be likely to increase the reliability of a marking system? Return to page *168* and choose another answer.

B *VIII 8a*

In this system a student would be assigned one of only three marks. This would result in a loss of considerable information and be relatively unreliable because there are so few categories. Return to page *170* and choose another answer.

A *VIII 5b 6*

Good! A mark put on a report card is frequently influenced by the teacher's opinion of the student's ability and attitude. As soon as this occurs the mark is not just a report of measurement but involves judgment as well.

There is considerable disagreement over the degree to which the marks assigned should reflect judgment. Is the teacher justified, for instance, in assigning different marks to two students who have received the same score on a unit test because one has an I.Q. of 130 and the other has an I.Q. of 90? Some would say they should receive different marks because this score may not be a very good score for a student with an I.Q. of 130. It may be a good score for a student with an I.Q. of 90. Others would say that they should not because the mark assigned should reflect only measurement (his score on the test) and not a judgment of how good or bad the score is.

Two students have the same number of points on tests and papers done during a nine-week period. The teacher gives one a *B* and the other a *C* because one student has shown a better attitude than the other. Under these conditions, the marks assigned reflect:

a. Measurement. (*P. 163B.*)

b. Judgment. (*P. 164B.*)

c. Both measurement and judgment. (*P. 168A.*)

B *VIII 8b*

This five-mark system would yield more reliable information than excellent, fair, and poor, but there is an even better answer than *A, B, C, D, F.* Return to page *170* and find it.

A *VIII 7b*

The factor or factors which form the basis for the judgments vary from one teacher to the next and probably for a given teacher from one time to another. Is such a poorly defined basis for judgment likely to increase the validity of a marking system? Return to page *168* and choose another answer.

B *VIII 9a*

A pass-and-fail system does make marking relatively easy but it gives up too much in reliability and results in the loss of too much information. Return to page *169* and choose another answer.

A *VIII 6c 7*

Correct! These marks reflect both measurement (scores on tests and papers) and judgment (how good the students' attitudes were).

There are a number of problems associated with mixing measurement and judgment in a marking system. One of the most serious has already been mentioned. That is the highly subjective and imprecise nature of most teacher judgments. It is difficult enough to develop a valid and reliable marking system based on measurement. It is virtually impossible to develop one where both measurement and judgment are involved. A related problem is that of the basis for the judgment. There are many factors related to achievement. Which of these is the teacher going to use in judging a student's achievement? Intelligence is obviously related to achievement, but so is social class and previous achievement in similar activities. Is a student's mark to be based on all the measurements we have on him plus some adjustment for each of these factors? If not all of them, which ones is it to be based on and how much of an adjustment is to be made for each? The difficulty in answering these questions, when combined with the subjectivity and imprecision involved in most teacher judgments, can have serious consequences for the validity and reliability of a marking system.

What effect does combining measurement and judgment have on the validity and reliability of a marking system?

a. It reduces validity but increases reliability. (*P. 165A.*)

b. It reduces reliability but increases validity. (*P. 167A.*)

c. It reduces both validity and reliability. (*P. 170A.*)

B *VIII 10a*

There is nothing magical about marking "on the curve." The tradition of giving relatively fewer *A's* and *F's* than *B's, C's* or *D's* is just that, tradition. Return to page *171* and choose another answer.

A

VIII 8c 9

Good! A 9-category system would yield more reliable information than either a 5- or 3-category system.

If accuracy continues to rise as the number of categories increases, it might seem a good idea to use a system with as many categories as possible. Two factors must be considered: First of all, the gain in accuracy decreases as the number of categories increases. There is a much larger gain when the number is increased from 6 to 9 than when it is increased from 9 to 12. Secondly, the more categories there are, the more difficult marking becomes. It is much easier to mark papers *pass* or *fail* than to mark them *A, B, C, D,* or *F.* Some compromise is required then between accuracy of mark and difficulty of marking. A 9- or 10-category system seems to represent a good compromise. There is not much gain in accuracy when the number of categories is increased beyond 9 or 10 and a 9- or 10-category system does not place an unreasonable marking burden on the teacher.

Which of the following marking systems would represent the best compromise between accuracy of mark and difficulty of marking?

1. Pass and fail. (*P. 167B.*)
2. A, B, C, D, E, F, G, and H. (*P. 171A.*)
3. 1, 2, 3, 4, 5, 6, 7, 8, 9, 10, 11, 12, 13, 14, 15, and 16. (*P. 172A.*)

B

VIII 11a

Under certain conditions the teacher might use these percentages but there is a better answer to the question. Return to page *173* and find it.

A

Right! Adding judgment to measurement is likely to have a negative effect on both the validity and the reliability of a scoring system.

A fourth question that arises relative to a marking system is how many and what type of marks to use. The point is sometimes made that the fewer the marks used the fewer the misclassifications. If only pass and fail are used the chance of putting a student in the wrong group is less than if a four-mark system such as excellent, good, fair, and poor is employed. This reasoning is correct as far as it goes. One serious problem with two- or three-mark systems, however, is loss of information. If 20 percent of the students are given a fail mark and 80 percent receive a pass mark, the mark of pass does not really tell very much about a student. A tremendous amount of information is lost between the measurement results which the teacher has and the mark assigned. Another serious problem is that related to the accuracy of the information provided by the mark. It is sometimes suggested that if the information available has relatively low reliability it is better to use fewer categories. Reducing the number of categories, however, also reduces the reliability of the mark assigned. This may seem illogical because there are obviously going to be fewer misclassifications if only two grades such as satisfactory and unsatisfactory are assigned than if a ten-point scale is used. It can be shown, however, that regardless of the reliability of the basis used to assign marks, the reliability of the mark assigned decreases as the number of categories used is reduced. Although the decrease in the reliability of the mark is less when the basis for marking has low reliability, we can never make a mark more accurate simply by reducing the number of categories used in the marking system.

Which of the following marking systems would yield the most reliable information, assuming a given reliability for the basis of assigning the mark?

a. Excellent, fair, poor. (*P. 165B.*)

b. A, B, C, D, F. (*P. 166B.*)

c. 1, 2, 3, 4, 5, 6, 7, 8, 9. (*P. 169A.*)

B

This might be the best way to apportion the marks for some students in some classes for some purposes. There is, however, a better answer. Return to page *173* and find it.

Correct! The pass-and-fail system gives up too much in accuracy while the 16-point system would present tremendous difficulties in marking. The 8-point *A-H* system seems the best compromise.

Once the decision about how many categories are to be used is made, some decision must be made about how these categories are to be defined. We must first of all be very clear about what scores tell us about a student. In and of themselves they tell us practically nothing. Typically, they take on meaning only when we know how one student's score compares with the scores of other students like him. To know that John Smith had a score of 42 on a test means very little until we know how that score compares with that of his classmates. Scores and the marks based on them then are basically indications of rank order. We must also recognize that there is no one best way to distribute students among the categories in a marking system. There is no reason to assume there must be fewer *A's* than *B's* or *B's* than *C's.* That we do, in fact, give fewer *A's* than *B's* or *B's* than *C's* is by tradition not by necessity.

A good marking system should be based on the normal curve with fewer *A's* and *F's* than *B's, C's* and *D's.*

a. True. (*P. 168B.*)

b. False. (*P. 173A.*)

A *VIII 9c*

This 16-point system would yield the most accurate information but would put a tremendous burden on the teacher. Return to page *169* and choose another answer.

B *VIII 12a 13*

You are right! The percentages are less ambiguous than the terms "good," "average," and "poor." They are also more in keeping with the nature of the data on which the mark is based.

One last issue in marking which might be discussed very briefly is whether the labels for the categories should be letters or numerals. At one time numerals were widely used. Numerals up to 100 were often used and interpreted as percentages. A 90 was, for instance, assumed to indicate 90 percent learning. Because of the difficulty of establishing what constituted 0 percent and 100 percent learning this use of numerals as percent of learning obviously had little validity. There was then a shift from numerals to letters. Letters have also been assigned properties which they do not in and of themselves possess. Whatever meaning the mark *A* has, it has because of tradition. Another disadvantage of letters is that they cannot be added and divided directly. If a student has marks of *C, A, C, B* these four marks must be converted to numerals, e.g., *2, 4, 2, 3* before they can be averaged. The use of numerals in the first place would remove the necessity for this extra step when averaging marks.

Which of the following sets of numerals would retain an advantage in averaging and at the same time be unlikely to be misinterpreted as percentages?

a. 1, 2, 3, 4, 5, 6, 7. (*P. 176A.*)

b. 65, 70, 75, 80, 85, 90, 95. (*P. 175A.*)

Good! There are a number of factors to be considered when deciding how to apportion students among the categories in a marking system. It should not be assumed that the normal curve is the best model to use under all or even most conditions.

Among the factors to be considered are the type of students enrolled in the course, the assignment being marked, and the use to be made of the mark which is given. If an *A, B, C, D,* and *F* system is used it might be advisable to give more *A's* in Chemistry than in General Science, in an accelerated class than in a remedial class, in daily work than on report cards. The important point to recognize is that the decision should be made after careful thought and consideration. It should not be made on the basis of tradition or the presumed magical properties associated with some model such as the normal curve.

If a teacher uses the *A, B, C, D,* and *F* system of marking approximately what percent of each should he assign?

a. 10% *A's*, 20% *B's*, 55% *C's*, 10% *D's*, and 5% *F's*. (*P. 169B.*)

b. 20% *A's*, 20% *B's*, 20% *C's*, 20% *D's*, and 20% *F's*. (*P. 170B.*)

c. There is no way to answer this question from the information given. (*P. 174A.*)

Right! The answer to the question depends on the type of class and students involved, the nature of the assignment being marked, and the purpose for marking. None of this information is provided.

The meaning of a mark, like the number of students who receive it, can be whatever the teacher chooses to make it. If the mark of 85 is consistently assigned to 40 percent of the students in a class it has a different meaning from what it would have were it assigned to 90 percent of the students in a class. Because the meaning of a mark changes as the basis for assigning it shifts, it is important that teachers be very explicit about what the marks they assign mean. When the marks used are letters or numbers, the definition given is often in the form of a single word or short phrase. For instance, *A* (superior), *B* (good), *C* (average), *D* (below average), *F* (failing.) The problem is that words such as "superior" and "average" are so vague. In addition, the tests used as a basis for the marking do not yield scores called superior, good, average, below average, and failing. They only rank order the students. Since the marking systems is based on this type of data, the definitions of the marks should also be in terms of relative standing. The words "superior," "good," "average," below average," and "failing" might, for instance, be replaced by "top 10 percent," "next 20 percent," "next 55 percent," "next 10 percent," "bottom 5 percent."

Which of the following would be the better way to explain the marks assigned in a three-category system?

a. 1 (upper 25%), 2 (middle 50%), 3 (lower 25%). (*P. 172B.*)

b. 1 (good), 2 (average), 3 (poor). (*P. 176B.*)

These values can be averaged as they are but they are also very likely to be misinterpreted as percentages. Return to page *172* and choose another answer.

A *VIII 12b*

The terms good, average, and poor are extremely vague and easily misunderstood. It would be much better if the marks *1, 2,* and *3* were defined in more concrete terms. Return to page *174* and choose another answer.

B *VIII 13a*

Good! These values can be averaged as they are, and they are unlikely to be misinterpreted as percentages.

You have now completed this short introduction to classroom testing. I hope it has been pleasant. More importantly, I hope it has given you a grasp not only of the mechanics of test construction but also of the total pattern of objectives, methods, testing, and grading. Neither this book nor another can, by itself, make you an expert item writer. This requires time and practice in addition to knowledge of certain principles of item construction. You are, however, now in a position to write better tests. How much better depends on your willingness to spend the time and effort required to write valid and reliable items.

RELATED TITLES

EVALUATING PUPIL GROWTH: PRINCIPLES OF TESTS AND MEASUREMENT THIRD EDITION

J. Stanley Ahmann and Marvin D. Glock

BEHAVORIAL OBJECTIVES AND INSTRUCTION

Robert J. Kibler, Larry L. Barker and David P. Miles

AN INTRODUCTION TO STATISTICS AND MEASUREMENT: A PROGRAMMED BOOK

Lowell A. Schoer

ALLYN AND BACON, INC.
470 ATLANTIC AVENUE
BOSTON, MASSACHUSETTS 02210

PER CENT 12

GRADE 5

ITEM 13 20